# THE PERFECTION
## *of*
# DANCE

Leonid Zhdanov
and
Margarita Yussim

COOMBE BOOKS

CLB 4043
This edition published 1994 by Coombe Books
© 1994 Copyright SARL, Paris
© 1994 English-language edition CLB Publishing,
Godalming, Surrey
All rights reserved
Printed and bound in China
ISBN 1-85833-299-0

*The Bolshoi theatre.*

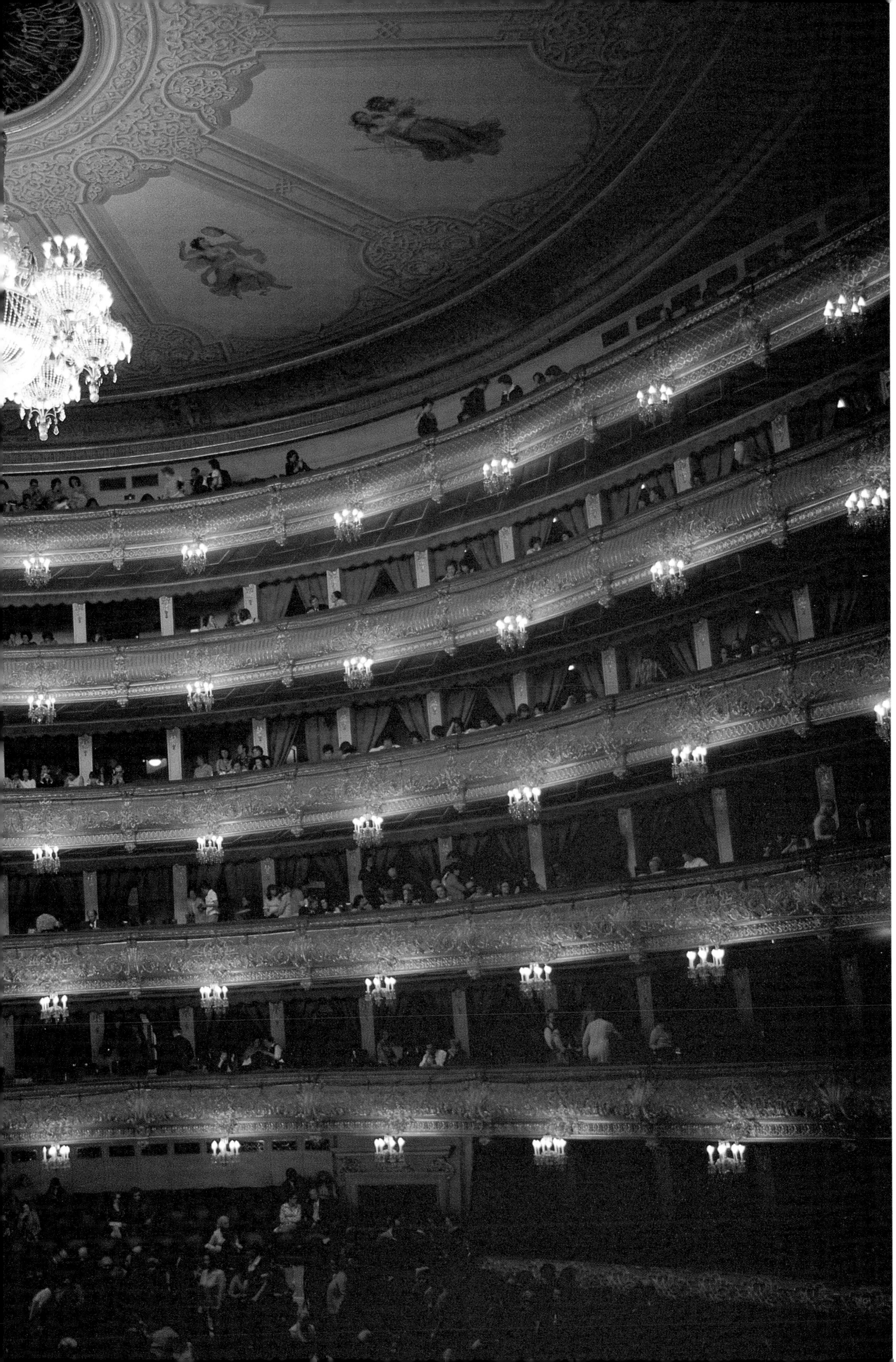

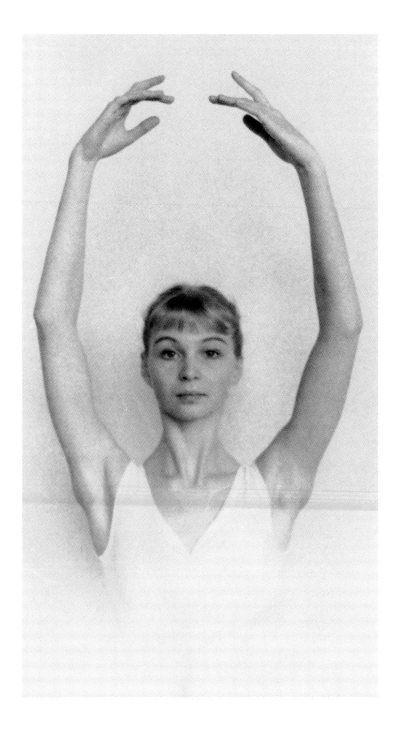

# CONTENTS

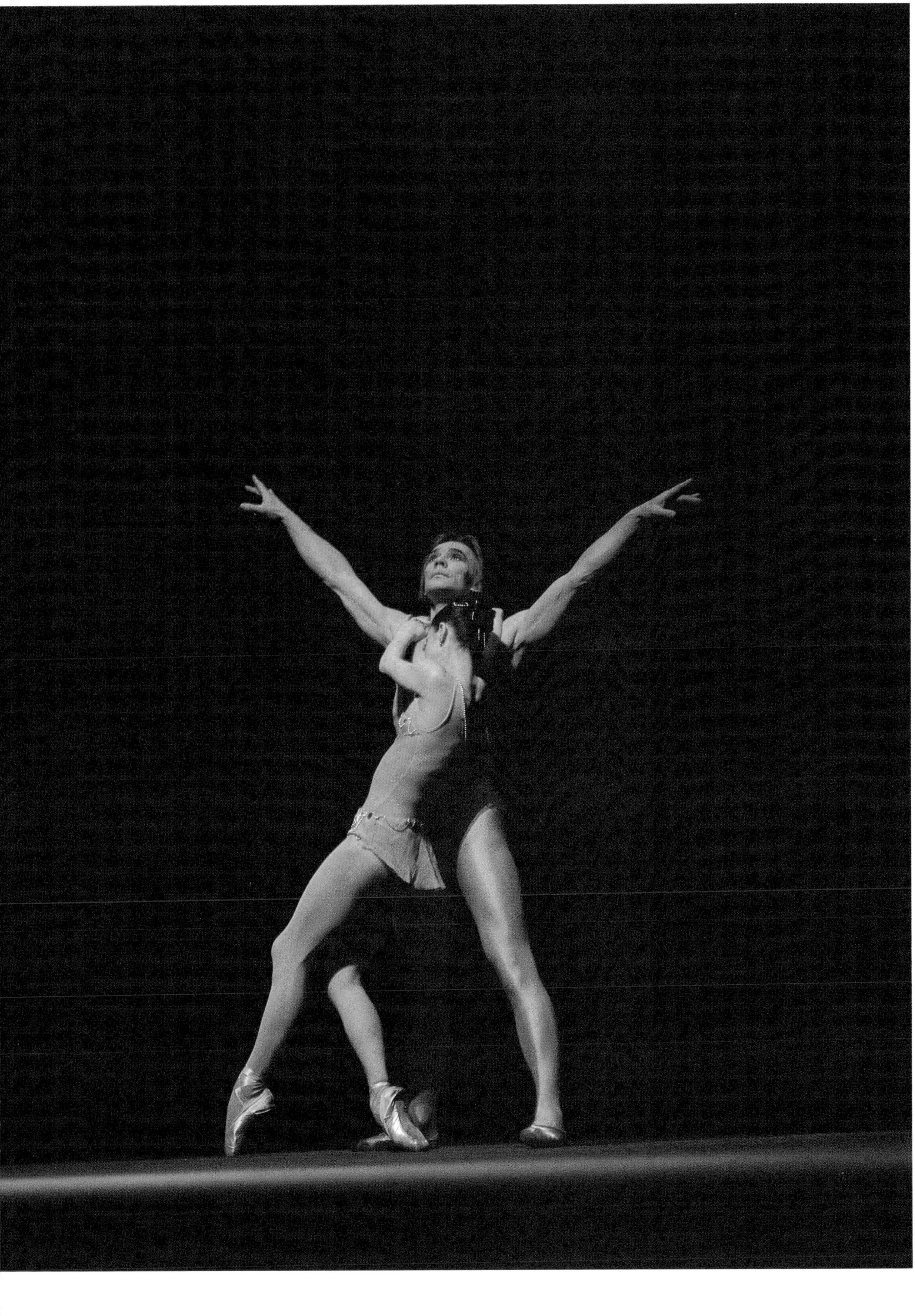

# THE PERFECTION
*of*
# DANCE

LEONID ZHDANOV

and

MARGARITA YUSSIM

# AN
# OCCUPATION
# AS
# DIVINE
# AS IT IS
# MYSTERIOUS

LUCIAN, 2ND CENTURY AD

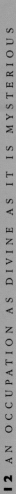

*In March 1978, Maurice Béjart's Ballet du XXe siècle appeared at the Bolshoi.*
*Shown here: Yekatarina Maximova and Jorge Don in a performance of "Romeo and Juliet", with music by Berlioz.*

*This shows one of those rare occasions when Maximova danced with a partner other than Vassilyev.*

The domain of Terpsichore, the youngest of the muses, became a separate art only a little more than three centuries ago. Every art is governed by its own professional laws, and the law of classical dance is expedience. The fundamental principle of the position of legs and feet, so judiciously refined in the past, has made it possible to broaden the naturally limited abilities of the human body by increasing the amplitude in the motion of the leg at the hip joint. The arms, the body and the head have also acquired a position which corresponds to this principle, but which is far removed from the natural human stance. The human body has come to be organized in a new way.

The anatomical structure of the arms and legs is different, and hence the difference in the techniques for their training in classical dance. Historically, the development of arm and leg training methods went different ways. The initial positions in the definition of their role and functions in classical dance were different, too. The training of feet in classical dance covered the path from expedience to beauty, from trade to art. But the training of arms, on the contrary, took a different direction: from beauty to expedience, from art to trade (or profession).

The first techniques of classical dance were developed by the first professional dancers, acrobats and jugglers of distant epochs. This is proven by numerous ancient vase paintings and frescoes which depict dancers with turned out feet.

If one sets out to look for equally convincing evidence of professional arm position in classical dance, the sources that can be found date from a later period: antique sculptures and works by Italian Renaissance artists.

For example, a fragment of Botticelli's famous painting *The Spring*, depicting the round dance of the Three Graces, gives a direct depiction of the contemporary dancing style. The central fresco of the Sistine Chapel by Michelangelo, showing scenes of the Last Judgment, can also give grounds for comparison between the outlines of its characters' arms with those adopted in classical dance. Both Botticelli and Michelangelo were undoubtedly familiar with the professional dance of their era. This might be the explanation for the professional, pulled-up torsos of the Three Graces in *The Spring* and even for the fact that they walk on half-toes, which makes the female figures still lighter. The dancers' arms too are involved in their movement; they are connected like a living garland.

If the dancers' figures are considered from the viewpoint of their leg, arm, body and head positions, we can also see some professional elements. Although the dancers' arms are not free but joined, their linear outline (the smooth roundedness of one lowered and the other raised arm with the elbows set aside from the face) are very reminiscent of today's preparatory and 3rd positions.

The arm outline in the *Last Judgment* scene also reminds one of the linear, visual principles of professional arm setup in classical dance. If the same point of view is taken toward the central figure of the Creator, whose arms are raised in a wrathful gesture of

*Roman replicas of Greek reliefs from the Hellenistic period, circa 2nd century BC. Bacchante dancing, with dulcimer.*

punishment, a classical shape close to the 1st and 3rd positions can be seen there too. Has the artist repeated the shapes he saw in professional dancers of his time? Or, amazingly, has art anticipated the birth of such shapes and lines in classical dance? What is most probable is that artists simply depicted their subjects the way they understood the beautiful: the widely spread shoulders, the high, proud line of the neck, the dignified position of the head, the strong yet smooth lines of the arms revealing a strength of character. This harmony, stability and balance of shapes and volumes, reflected the dignity of the classical sculpted image.

What forms the focus of the central Sistine Chapel fresco showing the Last Judgment is the gesture of the Creator, embodying supreme justice, assuring the spectator of his true existence. The expressiveness of that powerful and wilful gesture does not impair the harmonious balance of form. There is nothing in the arm lines that could be viewed as distorting, ugly, too sharp or insufficiently dignified; there is nothing to tip the balance of the body in motion. This appears to be the reason why the Creator's figure does not look too bulky despite his exaggeratedly strong, volcanic muscles. There is a feeling of invincible power emanating from that figure. The dialectical unity of two opposite beginnings – motion and rest, – underlies the artistic principles of the image. These are the same principles that govern the body positions in classical dance. This is what seems to have generated the linear, visual, artistic and aesthetic foundations of classical dance. It is true that "… the arts march forward with their hands joined. What is noticeable in one of them as an impressive but particular feature may become a permanent trait of another as time goes on …."[1]

Marina Semenova, a most "classical" ballerina and dance teacher, suggested that Greco-Roman and Renaissance art should be turned to in search of accurate stylistic guidance in the arm positions. "The shape of the arms should not only be worked on in class alone," she said. "Do study the works of Greco-Roman sculptors and Renaissance artists. There is a lot to learn from them …."

"… Marina Semenova said that when she was working on the shape of her arms and hands, she studied reproductions of Greco-Roman sculptures and pictures by Italian Renaissance artists."[2]

The significance which Renaissance artists attached to the depiction of arms and the depth of meaning which they gave to every gesture can be judged even from the few paintings by great masters that are given as illustrations in this book.

God's wrathful gesture of punishment in *The Last Judgement* is the centre of the fresco's emotional charge and meaning. It conveys very aptly the message of the whole painting.

In another fresco in the Sistine Chapel, the arms of the Creator and those of Adam the Progenitor, which they outstretch towards each other, tell the story of the Creation of Man and the

*Above: Niobide, Niobe's son, struck by Apollo's arrow.*

*Below: Fragment from Michelangelo's fresco of "The Great Flood".*

**1.** P. Karp. *Mladshaya Muza* (The Youngest Muse). Moscow, 1986, p.34.

**2.** Ye. Aksyonova. Klass M. T. Semenovoy v Bolshom Theatre (M. T. Semenova Class in Bolshoy Theatre). – In: *Voprosy Vospitaniya Baletmeisterov v Teatralnom VUZe (Questions of Teacher Training in a Theatrical College)*. Moscow, 1980, p.168.

magical mystery of the emergence of the human spirit. It looks as though Adam's body, which is ready for life but is so far dumb and sleeping, will come to life in another second. The energy of the picture is contained in the tips of God's and Adam's fingers.

As classical dance developed in time, the arms' role changed, too, both as a support and as an independent emotional, imaginative and expressive element. There are far more differences in their arm setup between different national dance schools than there are in their foot setup. There are more frequent deviations from tradition and the rules in the work of the arms than in the work of the legs. And this is understandable. The rigid system of leg and body position is the basis of classical dance techniques, ensuring stability in the most complex virtuoso movements. The legs and the trunk form the steelwork of the dance techniques. The smallest deviation from the rules of classical setup threatens to destroy the firmness of movement and to cause the performer to lose stability. The arms play a subordinate role in dance techniques: they serve as a support in the execution of virtuoso movements (like *fouettés*). But it is impossible to imagine a pose – the basis of expression in classical dance – without the involvement of arms. In the pose the arms play quite an independent and often dominating, meaningful role. The measure of arm involvement in the general structure of classical dance is determined by the required technical skill. The more

*A bacchante and a satyr.*
*Relief on a crater.*

virtuosity there is in a movement, the greater the assistance of the arms, which should be both active and accurate.

It is universally acknowledged that world ballet owes the Russian school the credit for the assertion of the great imaginative and artistic role of the arms in the general structure of classical dance, as well as the specific coordinating patterns determined by these movements.

The Russian school has changed the meaning and significance of arm movement from what used to be a framing embellishment of the general body outline and a crowning pattern intended only to please the eye, into a melody of form which is capable of producing piercingly tragic notes (such as in *Swan Lake* scenes), gentle sighs of hands (as in the choreographic ensembles of *Chaupiniana*), or sharply cutting and tragic rhythmic outcries (as in Mehmene-Bahnu's choreographic monologues from *The Legend of Love*).

According to Maya Plisetskaya, in *The Swan* by Saint-Saëns as put on stage by Michel Fokine for Anna Pavlova, the arms are leading the melody while the feet conduct the accompaniment. In other words, the arms can become the core of choreographic imagery in which the melodies of the composer's, choreogrpher's and performer's souls are merged.

Arm movements require far less physical effort from the performer than leg movements. Unlike the legs, whose movements require mathematical precision in direction to prevent the performer violating any of the rigid rules, the arms "... can be set

*Above: Raphael's "Triumph of Galateus". Fragment of fresco.*

*Left: "The Three Graces". Fragment from "The Spring" by Botticelli.*

*Below: Bacchic dance (bacchante playing a Pan flute with two satyrs).*

*Galina Oulanova in Fokine's "Chopiniana". In Western Europe, this ballet is better known as "Les Sylphides". Here, the dancer demonstrates the expressiveness of the arms. Whilst maintaining her feet in the 5th position, she is able to continually vary the arm movements.*

in one or another way … as they are that part of the skeleton which is the least involved in bodily restructuring."[1] This anatomical fact, which gives relative freedom to the arms, has two-fold consequences. On the one hand, it allows some deviation from the rules and threatens with amateurishness in performance. On the other, it gives a lot of room for the expression of the performer's inspiration and personal ego. This relative freedom in the expression of one's internal impulses through arm movements explains why the arm dances of many outstanding ballerinas are so different in intonation despite their basically uniform professional techniques. The arms of Marie Taglioni, Fanny Elssler, Anna Pavlova, Marina Semenova, Maya Plisetskaya, Yekaterina Maksimova and Natalya Bessmertnova make a whole world of colours, shapes, volumes and patterns creating unique timbres of dance tone. The beauty of that world consists in its variety and colourfulness.

The arm movements of every outstanding ballerina with a unique personality reveal a distinct note of her own, just as there is always a nuance of his own in the art of every great dramatic actor. The setup and bearing of the figure, the movements of the arms, are capable of disclosing an individuality and the pantomimic prototype akin to it.

Marina Semenova always conveys her own sense of classical dance, rooted in the majestic forms of Greco-Roman sculpture, even in those classical parts where the choreographer directs stylized arm patterns. In Minkus's *The Bayadere* she combined oriental stylistics with classically-rounded arms.

The gentle silhouette and fragile subtlety of the arms and figure of Galina Ulanova, another great ballerina of our times, are reminiscent of Botticelli's beautiful images.

Maya Plisetskaya's proud and strong body, her boldly spread arms, reveal the inner self of her heroines. Her gestures, like those of Greco-Roman statues, did not look like a masquerade but were born of an internal impulse as she turned to the image of Isadora Duncan.

But the sad and pitiful branch-like arms of Natalya Bessmertnova as *Giselle*, the ascetically thin and obediently-joined hands of her *Anastasia*, stemming from the iconic style of ancient Russian painting and the images of mourners, produce an entirely different image.

When creating a scenic image, talented choreographers have always found its sources both in some idea with which they were concerned and in the unique individuality of the performer. The more accurate the choreographer's instinctive choice, the more precisely can he reveal the performer's inner self and let the spectator enjoy the unique beauty of his or her natural plasticity. Arm dance plays a very important role in the creation of an artistic image in ballet.

The ballet director's fantasy and choreographic thinking can have as definite an impact on the ballet styles and techniques of

1. L. D. Blok. *Klassicheskiy Tanets. Istoriya i Sovremennost* (Classical Dance. History and Modern Times). Moscow, 1987, p.28.

*Galina Oulanova in "The Fountain of Bakhchisaray", choreography by R. Zakharov. She was the first dancer to perform the role of Marie in this ballet. This photo was taken during one of her last performances.*

his time as the individual interpretation of form of gifted performers. The choreographer and the performer are almost inseparable participants in a two-way process in which the styles and techniques characterizing their epoch become crystallized. Whose share in the process is greater is difficult and hardly necessary to define. Life always makes accents of its own in every individual case. When discussing *La Sylphide,* for example, an epoch-making ballet in the romanticist era, the romantic image of dancer Marie Taglioni comes to mind in the first place. Her gentle, ethereal and noiseless dance was what prompted choreographer Philippo Taglioni in the overall style of the ballet.

This style is based on the beauty of undertones and the poetry of uncertainty. The lack of visible effort, the noiselessness of soaring leaps, easy lifts to half-toes and inaudible step-downs to full feet, elongated arm and hands shapes in semi-*arabesques*, and the capricious curve in the neck line – all that supplied the image of an unreal, dreamy and fleeting creature.

When they talk about Petipa's ballets it is normally the monumental structure of his works that is implied. The style

*"The Dancing Camargo" by N. Lancret.*

created by Petipa is distinguished by the classical clarity and beauty of fulfilment and stability. It is detectable in the monumental designs of large choreographic ensembles and in the patterns of each solo part. The Petipa dance is poetry hailing the poses and positions of classical dance. It allows you to enjoy the beauty of the *attitude* pose by slowly and repeatedly rotating it like a statue on a pedestal with the help of the *tour lent* technique in an *adagio* with four men, and then in the final *adagio* performed in the triumphant apotheosis of *The Sleeping Beauty.* This slow triumph is as symbolic of his style as the royal bearing of Aurora's head and the rounded shapes of her arms in poses. Every outstanding choreographer leaves traits of his time in the dance worlds and civilizations he creates. You can find such traits in the works of M. Fokine, A. Gorsky, K. Goleizovsky, F. Lopukhov, L. Lavrovsky, V. Vainonen or Yu. Grigorovich in Russian ballet, and in the works of George Balanchine, Jerome Robbins, Roland Petit, Maurice Bejart, Pierre Lacotte, John Cranko, or Kenneth MacMillan in world ballet.

The image of the Sylphide was created by Philippo Taglioni with due account of Marie Taglioni's physique. Her slightly stooping shoulders, her excessively long arms and elongated proportions were the materials from which the heroine's moulded image as well as her chief pose were born, and became the *leitmotif* and linking element in the ballet's fabric. The performer's outlook was taken into account in designing the costume for the Sylphide – an ethereal, winged creature.

It was in a similar fashion that Jules Perrault saw his Giselle in Carlotta Grisi, Michel Fokine his Swan in Anna Pavlova, Kasian Goleizovsky his Joseph the Handsome in Vassily Yefimov, Fyodor Lopukhov his Ice Maiden in Olga Mungalova, Leonid Lavrovsky his

These old photos of the great Russian ballerina Anna Pavlova demonstrate the perfection of her poses. What appears to be her natural perfection is in reality the result of enormous labour, as this photo of the teacher Cheketti correcting Pavlova's arms, shows.

*Whilst the myths that have grown up around Vasslav Nijinski abound, there are in fact very few photos of this prodigious dancer who revolutionised ballet at the beginning of the 20th century. These photos show the inimitable plastic expression of his jeux de bras. He is shown here in "Sheherazade", as Zobeide's black slave, and as the young man in "Les Sylphides".*

*Vasslav Nijinski in "The Spectre of the Rose", with T. Karsavina as the young girl.*

The creative powers of the human mind are astonishing. From only seven notes, an enormous number of musical scores have been composed and written. And from only five foot positions and three arm positions, countless choreographies, and small- and large-scale ballets have emerged.

Below: Vassilyev and Maximova in "Don Quixote".

Right: Maximova in "Nathalie".

Bottom right: Maximova in "The Stone Flower", choreography by Yuri Grigorovich.

*Vassilyev during rehearsals for the ballet "Leila and Medjnoun", in the version choreographed by K. Goleizovski, which was performed at the Bolshoi in 1965.*

Shakespearean Juliet and Rostislav Zakharov his Pushkinian Maria in Galina Ulanova, Yuri Grigorovich his Lady of the Copper Mountain in Alla Osipnko, his Crassus in Marius Liepa, and his Anastasia in Natalya Bessmertnova.

In the formation and development of classical dance as a universal system, the starting point is the school, which is the "conveyor of an uninterrupted, centuries-long tradition."[1] The system of classical dance is not unchangeable. It lives and develops in time, and "history teaches that professional dance has never remained the same or equal to itself for long periods of time. Every remarkable era in the theatre and every outstanding talent bring new dance styles with them."[2]

The practical experiences of performers and the creative quest of choreographers serve as the driving force to develop and carry on further the system of classical dance and the dance art as a whole.

The measure, meaning and imaginative significance of arm involvement in the structure of classical dance were different at different states of its technical development. Every breakthrough in techniques demanded more active participation of the arms in movement and sometimes opened up new horizons for their expressive capabilities. With the emergence of the *pointe* there appeared new, expressive opportunities for the arms. The invention of the *arabesque* is linked with the airy dance of Marie Taglioni. That pose, in which the arms are outstretched forward and into a distance and the hands in the *allongé* position, brought forth a new linear design for the arm dance and put an end to the hitherto compulsory rule of rounded arms.

*Maya Plisetskaya in "Swan Lake" and, right, in "Isadora". These photos were taken fifteen years apart: 1963 and 1978. In one of his interviews, Béjart remarked that "Plisetskaya could dance Isadora but Isadora Duncan couldn't have danced Maya Plisetskaya."*

There were times in the history of world ballet when the over emphasis on technical skills and virtuoso movements affected the arm outline negatively. Excessive tension made the arms look clamped and lose their dignified outline. That led inevitably to a loss of classical purity based on harmony, dignity and beauty. Technical skills which showed no visible effort were then replaced by a strained, coarse, romping "10-horsepower" manner (in the definition of L.D. Blok) with open, swinging arm movements prior to rotations and athletically straightened elbows and wrists. Increased virtuosity is in no way a negative phenomenon. But "overdoing it" technically may destroy the fabric of classical dance if it is at variance with artistry and becomes an end in itself. It was characterized very aptly by Joste Svalberg, Director of the Swedish Ballet School at the Royal Opera: "If ... the art of ballet is going to develop by building up new tricks, I am sorry for our common achievements in that art."

It is well known how enthusiastically modern dancers undertake the inclusion of technical tricks in their parts. But fewer performers are really concerned about such "trifles" as hand

---

**1.** Quoted from L. D. Blok. *Klassicheskiy Tanets* (Classical Dance). p.63.
**2.** Ibid., p.93.

outlines, arm patterns, or head bends and turns, all of which are elements of choreographic culture. They often lose that "tiny little bit" which belongs to the mystery of art. Ballet characters who are entirely different in style and by time of creation tend to lose their distinctive features, and heroes and heroines become disappointingly alike. It is sometimes hard to see a difference between Masha's dance from *The Nutcracker* and Aurora's dance from *The Sleeping Beauty,* the dances of Odette and Odile, the dance of Laurencia and that of Quitrie. What we see is a sterile, ascetic, neutral and unaddressed manner which may have something to do with classical dance, but does not add anything to the dance of some concrete character. This was partly the reason why some modern performers found it hard to grasp the unique style of *The Sleeping Beauty,* although it does not look like a work created a very long time ago. Irina Kolpakova, Yekaterina Maksimova and Lyudmila Semenyaka have set the standard for stylistic accuracy in Aurora's part, most manifest in some details which refer to arm and body movements.

Styles and techniques change in time, and the transformations of style can best be seen by comparing different dancers who played the same character at different times. While it is true that technical skills have improved progressively, the same is not true of style. A retrospective view can help detect some losses as well as victories. The designs, line and shapes of classical dancers' arms are imbued with not only the aroma of their times, but also with the unique qualities that creative personalities contribute to the art of classical dance. The design of poses can help us to follow the development of such characters as the Sylphide, Giselle, Aurora or Odette in time. It is impossible to say which is better: the Giselle of Carlotta Grisi or Natalya Bessmertnova, of Olga Spesivtseva or Galina Ulanova, the Aurora of Carlotta Briansa, the first performer, or of Irina Kolpakova, the Odette of Pierina Legnani or Maya Plisetskaya. They are all different, each one is unique, and each belongs to her time.

The variety of colours in classical dance arm movements is almost unlimited. A gesture can convey many messages, such as the drama of scenic action, the fine psychological nuances of emotional impulses, distinctive features of the time and nation. The richness of variations in arm movements combined with those of the legs, body and head is what gives birth to the style of a choreographic work and the individual visual form of every performer. Mastering style is a matter requiring a lot of artistic intuition and the ability to melt down one's experiences in life into creative images.

The precision of individual style does not depend on one's natural talent alone, but also on one's general cultural standard and intellect. There is nothing to promote a dancer's professional way of thinking like his or her familiarity with different choreographic styles and manners. And, of course, a ballet dancer is best formed by his or her thorough knowledge of the "roots": the classical heritage embodying the highest achievements of the ballet of previous epochs.

*These sketches are by the choreographer Kazein Goleizovski. He was over seventy when he put the finishing touches to his ballet "Leila and Medjnoun", and no longer able to demonstrate the plastic interpretation he wanted, he resorted to drawing it.*

The ballet theatre of the world knows some performers who have universal stylistic skills. Although they have a distinct intonation of their own, they can easily write themselves into any style. Such were some dancers of Michel Fokine's theatre: Anna Pavlova, Tamara Karsavina, Vaslav Nijinsky. Talking of the 1950s and 1960s in world ballet, one can name Yvette Chauviré in France, Margot Fonteyn in Britain, Marsia Heide in Germany, Carla Fracci in Italy, or Pieter Schaufuss in Sweden. Outstanding contemporaries Rudolf Nureyev, Natalya Makarova and Mikhail Baryshnikov, who now belong, or lately belonged, to the world's ballet theatre, have preserved a distinct Russian accent in adopting the styles of outstanding choreographers of the world.

Some outstanding choreographers and performers who are known as subtle stylists in modern dance are consistent in including classical masterpieces in their theatrical and concert repertoires, such as the works of Auguste Bournonville, Philippo Taglioni, Michel Fokine and Alexander Gorsky. Among them are Pierre Lacotte and Guilen Tesmard.

Those who are interested in ancient choreography are as a rule more efficient in mastering its opposite – the style of modern dance – and can give interesting interpretations to it. Moreover, the art of many talented performers who belong to different generations reveals a desire to combine the two opposites – ancient romantic choreography and modern dance. When such polar artistic trends co-exist in one performer's art, it should not be qualified as lack of either principle or discrimination. It is, rather, a manifestation of natural hunger for variety, of the desire to break up out-dated stylistic limits and escape the danger of clichés. Maya Plisetskaya, who had danced classical roles all her life, did not hesitate to take up the choreography of A. Alonso, M. Bejart and R. Petit. Yekaterina Maksimova, the most "classical" ballerina of the 1960s, came into contact with the ancient choreography of A. Bournonville and mastered the modern styles of T. Schiling, D. Briantsev, and M. Bejart.

In Maya Plisetskaya's repertoire of recent years, *The Swan Lake* was next to R. Petit's *Death of the Rose,* and *Don Quixote* with A. Alonso's *Carmen* and M. Bejart's *Bolero.*

Yekaterina Maksimova's repertoire includes A. Bournonville's *Natalie, ou La Laitière Suisse,* D. Briantsev's *Galatea,* M. Bejart's *Romeo and Julia.*

The opportunity to employ vaster layers of choreographic heritage gave a second breath to many performers and directors, a new awareness of themselves in art and of their capabilities on the ballet stage.

New horizons of art are associated with new themes and non-standard means of their implementation. New visual and rhythmic accents, unusual brushstrokes in the movements of the arms, legs, body and head stimulate the artist's creative quest. That paves the way for a new look on dancers' individualities in both modern and classical repertoire.

It is interesting to analyze the interpretation of modern styles by such a well-known classical dance master as Maya Plisetskaya. In classical ballet, while preserving the classical forms and lines of the body, arms and legs, she seems to have exceeded the limits of pure canonicity. What impresses the spectator in her modern choreographic works is not only her organic manner and freedom in performing unusual movements, but also formal clarity and the absence of any amorphous or uncertain stances. Plisetskaya's expressionist, spontaneous Bacchic undertones which break through in her classical parts as affecting the shapes, lines and movements of her arms, acquire classical qualities in her modern-dance repertoire. The arms of her Odette, the bird girl beating her wings desperately or sailing on rocking waves along the surface of the swan lake, and the arms of her Raymonda, whose movements seem to be knitting a fantastic ornamental design, break up from the inside the unquestionably austere ascetic form of the classical canon. The result is the beautiful professional "heresy" which only such big talents as Plisetskaya can afford.

In her modern repertoire, despite the anti-classical arm line of her Rose or the athletic gestures of her Isadora, Plisetskaya observes well-defined rhythmic and graphical organization in her arm movements, which is undoubtedly the result of her classical training and gives out her "classical origin."

It is a widely held view that a dancer's arms are enough to judge about his or her schooling standard and degree of traditionalism. It is equally true to say that the scope of a dancer's talent is manifested in his or her attitude to the elaboration of the arms score in this or that part. Given this, there can be different ways of emotional impact on the spectator. Every performer will make more use of those techniques which are closer to his or her individuality and temperament. Ulanova, for example, is a master of subtle strokes and expressive detail. If one analyzes her arm movements in any part, it is striking what austere, expressive means she used to produce a very strong emotional impression on the spectators. She may set out an index finger a little farther than required by the classical canon or make a slightly sharper turn of her back-drawn head – and here are the finishing touches to the portrait of Polish beauty Maria from *The Bakhchisarai Fountain* in the happy days of her serene youth. This barely noticeable detail of form points to the age and nationality of the heroine, and also

*These photos demonstrate particularly well the differences in choreographic writing between artists who all came out of the same tradition of the Russian school. Each of them discovered their own plastic independence. The first two photos, below, show rehearsals for the ballet "Leila and Medjnoun" by K. Goleizovsi, with Raissa Stroutchkova and V. Vassilyev.*

The other photos show rehearsals
for "The Stone Flower"
by J. Grigorovich, with
S. Alderkhayeva and V. Vassilyev.

*The ballet "Icarus", with Yekaterina Maximova and V. Vassilyev in a version choreographed by Vassilyev. Vassilyev, the dancer, came out of the confines of the Russian school, characterised by the traditional arm and leg techniques.*

conveys the emotional tenor of her state of mind. Many enthusiastic pages have been written about the expressive and accurate "play" of Ulanova's arm in the culmination scene of Maria's death. And indeed, Ulanova as the dying Maria whose hand slides down the column is no less striking than the most expressive details of paintings by the old masters. It is perceived by the audience as a sad sigh of farewell and quiet protest-free withdrawal from life in bondage.

While Ulanova gives preference to a sculpted hint, Marina Semenova can be called a master of sculpture in ballet. The marble of her arms, shoulders, torso and majestic head is what makes her Odete, Nicia, Aurora or Giselle stand out. Her art is characterized by the sculptural integrity of her scenic portraits. The positions of her arms, hands and fingers are sculpturally finished and complete at every moment of her dance, quite in line with the recommendations of classical choreographers.

Plisetskaya is an artist with rich brushstrokes. The expressive paintings of Plisetskaya's dance can be best witnessed in the incomparable arms of her Odette, Aurora, Quitrie, Raymonda, Zarema, Mehmene-Bahnu, Carmen or Swan (the latter as staged by Fokine).

*Vassilyev, the choreographer, found his personal expression in the style initiated by Goleizovski.*

It might appear that expressive arms are the attribute and privilege of female dance alone. But there are a lot of examples in Russian ballet, showing the significance of arm movements and patterns in male classical dance. If you look at the pictures of dancers from different generations – V. Nijinsky, A. Jermolayev, V. Vassilyev, M. Baryshnikov or R. Nureyev, reproduced in this book – you can watch the transformation of male execution styles in time and see how important for that process the arms' expressive capabilities were in male dance.

The inspired poses of Nijinsky as the Slave in *Scheherezade,* the Marquis from *Armida's Pavilion,* or the Youth in *Chaupiniana,* in which the details of body and arm movements played an essential role, are extremely expressive and emotional; they also give accurate ethnic characteristics and are incomparable in terms of their unique plasticity.

The new heroic intonation in male performance, brought forth by the heroes of Alexei Yermolayev, was largely based on his arm movements and lines. The powerful impulse and strong will readable in the arms of his Philip in *The Flame of Paris,* the devil-may-care gestures of bandit Severyan in *The Stone Flower,* or his cruel, aggressive, crooked hands as Tybald – all of these were new and previously unknown motifs in the ballet theatre.

His contemporary K. Sergeyev's arm movements are contrastingly lyrical and comparable to a tenor voice. Their intonation is determined both by his soft landings and by the general structure of his dance characterized by soft, rounded arm gestures.

The uniqueness of V. Vassilyev, who seemed to have no technical difficulties, consists in the absolute lack of limit to his expressive capabilities. His arms can convey an infinite variety of emotional signs: warmth and cantillation in the gestures of Russian heroes Ivanushka and Danila, intricate ornamentation in the arms of Mejnun, the hero of an Oriental legend, heroic inspiration and a call for exploits in the arms of Spartacus, or vibration and exhaustion in the arms and body of Narcissus.

*Mario Liepa in a performance of "Mozart" by V. Vassilyev.*

Each time the dancer reveals the gift of penetrating the choreographer's mentality and original intention to imbue his hero with exactly these features.

As one thinks of Vassilyev's dance, one is reminded of the words said about music by the great Spanish singer Montserrat Caballé: "Music at large is universal. It touches upon all themes and is accessible to everybody. At any rate, I sing for everybody and I think that music must be perceived as life. One must live it through and feel it flow down your veins like blood."[1]

This is how Vassilyev dances: not only with his body, but with his heart and blood. His arms, too, play an important role in creating this impression.

Ballet school students must learn the ABCs of arm, leg, body and head setup firmly and unshakably, so that it can serve as the professional ground for bright, scenic images to grow on. The path from the class to the stage is as irreversible as the need is obvious for a return from the stage to the school. This is the magic closed circle of the art of classical dance and its professional foundation. It is not accidental that after dancing an evening performance, the most glorious ballerinas will hurry to the exercise class the next morning to tune their bodily instrument and perfect the shapes of their arms and legs. Not surprisingly, Anna Pavlova took regular lessons from Maestro Cecchetti even when her fame was world-wide.

Liepa as the prince in "Swan Lake" and as Crassus in "Spartacus". Note the striking contrast between the traditional arm positions of "Mozart" and "Swan Lake" compared to those in the ballet "Spartacus".

The present work is a modest attempt to see our today's professional reflection in the strict mirror of the school and to remind the reader of the fact that work on arms in the schoolteacher's practice is a most subtle and serious area requiring patience, refined artistic thinking, erudition, intellect, accurate vision and, most importantly, an understanding of its significance in training and its high destination in the art of classical dance.

*Two generations: Galina Oulanova passes on her knowledge and her "being" to Maximova and Vassilyev. Rehearsal for the ballet "Giselle". Undeniably, this is where the strength of the tradition in Russian art and dance comes from: being passed down from artist to artist.*

*Maya Plisetskaya at the barre.*
*Last night she was the heroine of the ballet, bathed in the spotlights and caressed by the*
*cheers of an approving public. This morning, she is a docile pupil in the hands of her*
*teacher. And that is how it is every day. Once, when asked how long she had been studying*
*dance, Plisetskaya replied: "Nine years to start with, then for the rest of my life."*

V. Vassilyev in a dance class.
Rehearsal directed by A. Ermolaev.

Right: "Sheherazade" performed
by the Bakou Ballet.

# HAND
# TRAINING

**Work at the barre.**

The hand is the termination of the arm outline; it is what makes the arm dimensionally complete. The forms of the hand and finger movements in classical dance are naturally and organically connected with the lines and movements of the whole arm.

"The leading role in the movement of the arms as they go from one position to another, or as they are opened or closed, is played by the hands. They give a colouring and direction to the whole movement, and concentrate in themselves the whole life of the arms," writes N.I. Tarasov.[1]

A gesture can be made particularly expressive by some barely visible but very important movements of the hand and fingers. A well-set hand adds beauty to the dance and is of great help to the dancer. According to N.I. Tarasov, "… the hand, just like the eyes, gives the gesture in dance the necessary meaning and plastic finalization."[2]

In classical dance there are two major hand positions depending on the general arm outline in fixed positions and poses: *arrondi*, or rounded (*table 1, photos 1, 3*) and *allongé*, or elongated (*photos 2, 4*).

The *arrondi* principle is a fundamental one in the training of the arms. The rounded line of fingers in positions is associated with the general roundness of the whole arm.

In the initial phases of training the fingers should be held together so that the middle finger is rounded a little more than the rest, the thumb touches the side of the second phalanx of the middle finger, while the index and the little finger are rounded a little less than the middle finger (*photos 1, 3*).

The middle finger and the thumb organize the hand's shape. The middle finger gives direction to gestures and must always be visible.

The thumb should be straightened and directed to the middle finger. This position of the thumb makes the hand seem narrow. The thumb is the hardest digit to discipline when training the hands. It tends either to be held apart or bends towards the middle of the hand (*table 2b upper*). To discipline the hand, E.P. Gerdt recommended that children should be given a coin to hold between the thumb and the middle finger at the very beginning. This helps them organize the hand while leaving all the fingers except the thumb and the middle one free and unstrained.

When held together correctly, the fingers should not be joined tightly, but with a slight clearance between them, and each should be distinctly visible from all points of view. This gives the hand an air of lightness and delicacy. This grouping of fingers helps to make the hands look organized and

**TABLE 1**

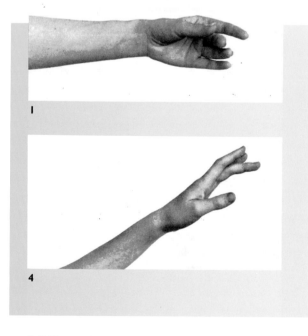

1

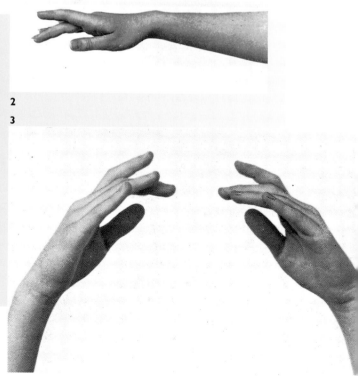

2
3

4

1. V. Morits, N. Tarasov, A. Chekrygin. *Metodika Klassicheskogo Trenazha* (Techniques of Classical Dance Training). Moscow-Leningrad, 1940, p.14.

2. N.I. Tarasov. *Klassicheskiy Tanets* (Classical Dance), p.180.

**TABLE 2**

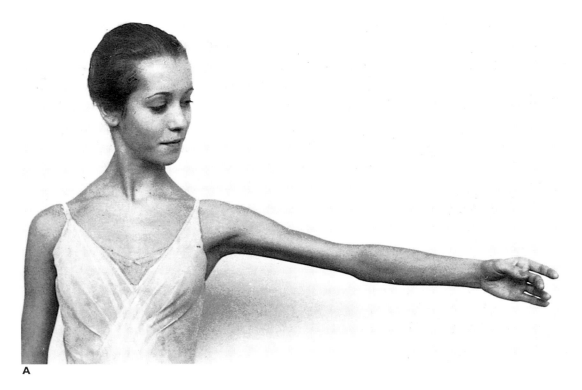

A

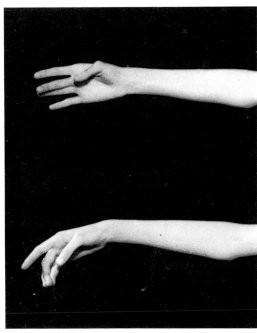

B

graceful without apparent strain or tension. Later the fingers will naturally depart from this initial setting, which seems somewhat affected, but in junior classes it is in exactly this way that the trainees should be taught to hold their hands in positions.

Apart from their fixed placement in positions, the fingers also participate in all the arm movements, but it is hardly possible to define the positions of the hands that should accompany all the movements because they change all the time. Such an attempt has, however, been undertaken in dance teaching theory. A classical dance training curriculum dated 1936 specified two main positions of the hand: "finger position in training" and "scenic finger position." The latter position corresponds to the hand shape for positions taught in intermediate and senior classes.

The second basic hand position accompanying the *allongé* and *arabesque* poses differs from the first one in that the hand has an elongated shape, just like the whole arm whose line it continues: without impairing the above described grouping, the fingers are opened to their entire length; they are not outstretched but straightened so that the third finger is visible and the tips of the index and small finger are set apart slightly above the middle and fourth fingers *(table 1, photos 2, 4)*.

Introduction of the *allongé* hand position comes at the moment when the arms are opened from the 2nd position before they are lowered into the preparatory stance. During the transfer of the arm from the 2nd position into an *allongé* the fingers are opened to their entire length, the palm is turned downward in a very economical movement, and the hand and fingers make a kind of "sigh" before being lowered into the preparatory position.

In all the positions and poses the hand is held at the same level as the forearm *(table 2a)*. The hand should not droop nor go up and break the arm line *(table 2b)*. The fingers should not be allowed to stretch out to the limit, because in that case the hand looks strained and pointed and makes the movements seem grotesque.

Arm training is a long process. The greatest difficulty in working on arms and hands is the need for precision in distributing the efforts needed for simultaneous arm and leg movements. Contrasting physical exertions and the confusing effects of the spatial and rhythmic patterns formed by combined arm and leg movement affect the shape of the hand first, causing it to be clamped and strained or to mirror the rhythmic and graphical patterns of the feet. Persistent and unremitting efforts are necessary in training the hand to be free and independent from trunk and leg motion from the very moment when arm movements begin to be included in exercises. This is one of the hardest tasks of the teacher.

Hand training is the subtlest part of the work on arms. It should start from the very first lessons and be given a special place in the training practice.

The theory of dance teaching includes different approaches to hand training at the initial stages. N.I. Tarasov believes, for example, that the hand should be trained together with the training of the arms' preparatory position in the middle of the floor. From the starting position (the feet in semi-turnout position I, the arms are down in a free manner on the sides of the body – *table 3, photo 1)*, the hand, being rounded from the fingers, takes the above described curved shape and this shape is fixed *(photo 3)*. Then the fingers are relaxed and return to the starting position *(photo 1)*. The exercise can be repeated several times and done periodically during the lesson. This approach helps the trainee develop a sense of the hand and the arm as of one whole from the very first lessons.

There is another known hand training technique employed by junior class teachers during the first lessons. From the starting position (the arms are down on the sides and relaxed), the hands are rounded slightly so that they do not touch the body along their entire length, and the fingers are put together in the above described manner. This isolates the hand setting technique as a task by itself without connecting it from the very beginning to the positioning of the arms, and can be used for several days.

1. A.Ya. Vaganova. *Osnovy Klassicheskogo Tantsa* (Fundamentals of Classical Dance). Leningrad, 1980, p.53.

TABLE 3

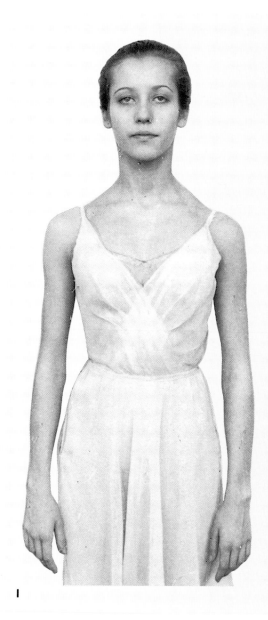

1

In the opinion of A. Vaganoa, "… it is only possible to show the precise manner of holding the hand by a vivid example during the lesson."[1] Yet explanation should also go naturally with it. The hands should be positioned meticulously, to the minutest detail; the grouping of fingers should be trained with due consideration of the pupils' differing physical shapes. In order that a pupil may visually check and control the position of each finger, he or she can be permitted, in the early stages of hand training, to hold the hand at a visible level outside all positions. It can also be helpful in making detailed explanations and can be recommended to pupils as a home task.

If the hand is to be light and vivid in all the arm movements, with a good balance of control and expression, it is necessary to train the smallest finger joints. L.M. Lavovsky recommended that performers

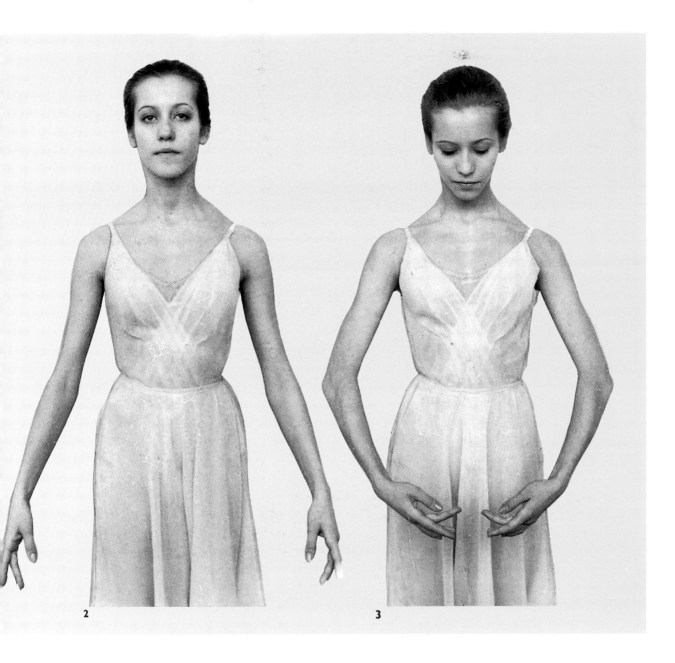

2

3

should be taught to feel their nail tips during their arm movements. This advice by a master and expert in classical dance is valuable in that it helps develop the sensitivity of the hand's small joints and ligaments. It also helps one attain the necessary measure in some barely noticeable movements of fingers which give additional life and "breath" to the hand and arm.

Experienced teachers look for and find their own techniques in teaching their pupils to develop an expressive, handsome and well-shaped hand. In order to prevent a tight hand and clamped fingers, for example, N.V. Zolotova of the Moscow Academic School, an experienced pedagogue, has recommended the following exercise. From the *arrondi* position the fingers are straightened and then slightly rounded again to regain the

starting position. The unbending movement should be felt to begin from the nail tips, and the bending movement from the cushions of the fingers. The exercise can be performed in all positions, but initially it should be trained in the 1st position because it is thus easier to control the precision of its execution. Though devoid of outward effect, the exercise helps remove tension from the smallest and thinnest hand joints and train their flexibility and docility, which is particularly important in training arm positions when the students have to hold their arms in static positions for a long time. Also, the exercise described helps develop the ability to begin a hand movement from the finger tips, which is later necessary in *port de bras*.

# CARRIAGE OF THE HEAD

Moscow 1974: N. Bessmertnova in "Giselle".

A teacher at the Bolshoi Academy of Dance.

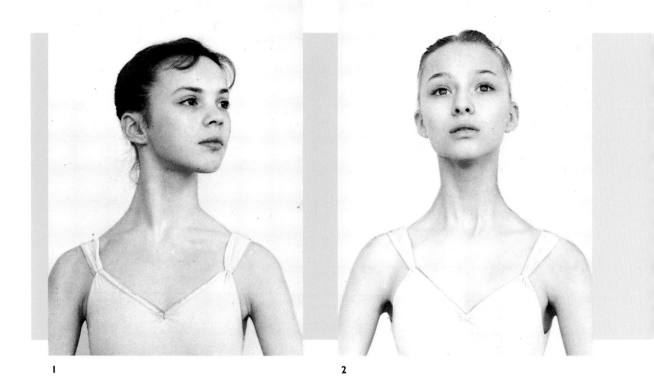

1

2

Arm training is closely connected with adequate bearing and therefore with the positioning of the head.

First of all, the head must be put exactly in the *en face* position. The neck line must be straight, high and unstrained, the chin must be even and upright, and the back of the head must be slightly behind the shoulder line.

Children often tend to stretch out their necks and chins, or to hug their necks in, with their heads too far back and the chins down. It is necessary to watch the correct position of the head.

From the *en face* position the head can turn into a profile or be slightly inclined or turned in various ways. Later the head and the eyes will participate in all the movements of the arms.

So that the children realize it is not only the legs but the entire body that is involved in classical dance, head positioning should be practised along with the training of the back and arms. "Systematic exercises for the head remove restraints from the neck muscles and give freedom to the movements of the head irrespective of the physical movement of the legs,"[1]

Ye. P. Gerdt said. "This is why Ye. P. Gerdt would start by meticulous work on the inclinations, turns and transfers of the head from one position to another," says S. Kholfina in a description of her arm and coordination training techniques.[2]

Given in this book are some exercises for the head which Ye. P. Gerdt would

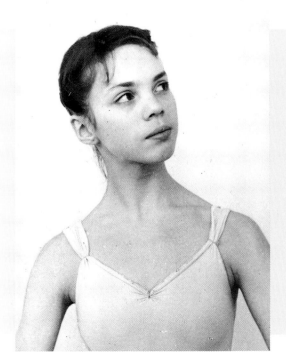

4

1. *Bulletin Metodkabineta MAKhU* (Bulletin of MAKhU Teaching Methods Division), No. 1. Moscow, 1958/59, p. 53.

2. Ibid.

3. *Bulletin Metodkabineta MAKhU* (Bulletin of MAKhU Teaching Methods Division), No. 1. Moscow, 1958/59, p. 53.

**3**

include as compulsory in her junior class lessons at the same time with arm training *(Table 4, photos 1-6)*. One can see from these examples how even the simplest turns, inclinations and transfers of the head are accompanied by the look of the eyes, a certain mood, artistry, grace and a sense of dance.

If carried out correctly, thorough head training provides the ground for the complex co-ordination of future virtuoso movements. "It is only possible to achieve complex co-ordination in intermediate and senior level classes if the pupils have gone through a good junior class training and can transfer their heads to this or that position with ease and without neck or face muscle tension. I know from experience that if the junior class teacher 'forgets' to include the head in the exercises at the bar and in the middle, his or her pupil will always be doomed to 'headless' dancing: her head will interfere with her poses, revolutions etc. And, on the contrary, a pupil taught from a very early age to turn, raise or lower her head in a free and easy manner will always co-ordinate the movements of her head with those of the arms, legs and body in a most natural way."[3]

## Positions

Arm positions are the official patterns of the arms accepted in classical dance. They form the basic element of professional aptitude and determine the uniformity of performance. All the movements of classical dance are performed strictly in and through the positions. The relocation of the arms from one position to another is what constitutes arm dance as such, in which the body, the head and the eyes are involved in a harmonious unity of motion.

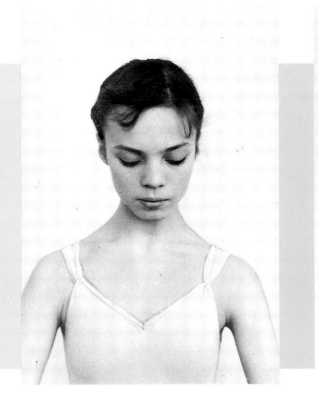

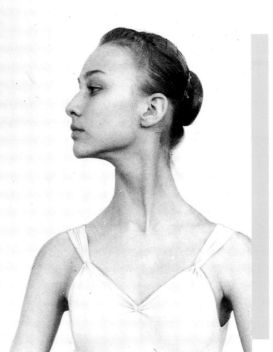

**5**

**6**

TABLE 5

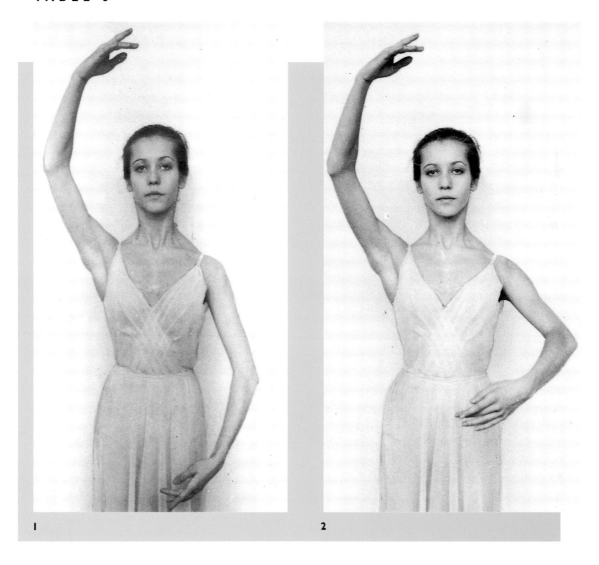

1

2

The arm positions, just like the positions of the feet, became established in practical choreography in France at the end of the 17th century. Their invention is credited to Pierre Beauchamp, a dancer and choreographer at King Louis XIV's court.

The position principle has remained unshakable from its very inception and still constitutes the foundation of professional skills, although the numbering of positions as well as their patterns have gone through considerable changes as choreography has developed. The Russian school played a special part in transforming the lines of arm positions and, more significantly, in the interpretation of their role in classical dance.

The patterns accepted in the Russian school of classical ballet are marked by clarity, simplicity and dignity; and the principle of smooth roundedness gives them additional span and ease.

The purity of lines, precision of their pattern and a measure of artistry strictly conforming with the student's age are the primary objects of arm position training.

Experienced teachers believe that it is precisely in the work on arms that the teacher's personality, talent and taste play a great role. Says Yelizaveta Pavlovna Gerdt: "There exists the canonical shape of arms in the positions, but every teacher adds some new detail, something of his own to that seemingly rigid framework, which is what constitutes his or her individual manner and style of teaching."[1] She herself had the ultimate knowledge of forming style and the ability to teach her pupils to execute the arm positions with all the purity of lines, but without losing their inherent natural grace.

In setting the positions of the arms, just like those of the feet, the head and the body, it is necessary to take full account of the pupil's constitutional and physiological setup. For example, if the arms are excessively long, they should be rounded at the elbow to a slightly greater extent in all the positions. Or if the arms are too short, the circular and elliptical shapes in the 1st and 3rd positions can be a little more

1. *Bulletin Metodkabineta MAKbU* (Bulletin of MAKhU Teaching Methods Division), No. 1. Moscow, 1958/59, p. 53.

elongated, while in the 3rd and preparatory positions the arms can be parted to a slightly greater distance than normally.

When training the arms, the pupils should be given explanations about the mechanism of the right bearing (i.e. about how and with what muscles the arms can be held in the correct position). The model they should be working for should be shown and explained to them.

Law number one in the positioning of the arms is their "separation" from the body. In all the positions the arms should be fixed in the shoulder joint in the correct position which allows them to move independently of the shoulders.

In the initial phase of training the position should be checked in the mirror when standing *en face*. Later it should come to include the look of the eyes, and the turns and inclinations of the head, so that the elementary postures may acquire meaning and expression.

When practising circular positions (preparatory, 1st and 3rd) it is recommended that the pupils understand the concept of the central vertical line, one dividing the performer's figure in half *(Table 5, photos 1, 2)* and also the fact that in none of the circular positions should the arm cross this line *(photos 1a, 2b)* or depart aside from it *(photos 1b, 2a)*. The right arm moves in the right half, and the left arm in

IA

2B

2A

IB

the left half. Later emphasis on this rule will help preserve the purity of arm positions in poses and their correct shape in rotations.

There used to be seven arm positions in the Russian school of classical dance. Only three plus the preparatory position are recognized today *(Table 6, photos 1-4, 1a-4a).* The three-position approach, introduced by A. Vaganova, considers all other arm postures as combinations of the basic three.

In all the positions the shoulders should be well straightened, the arms slightly bent to a smoothly rounded shape and the elbow point unnoticeable.

The mastering of arm positions includes formation of the correct line, attainment of the right level to hold the arms, finger groupings and closing distances between the hands in the 1st, 3rd and preparatory positions.

In all the positions it is the muscles of the shoulder, the forearm and the thoroughly lowered shoulder blades that put the arms where they should be.

Practical teaching in junior classes has shown that it is extremely difficult initially to get the positions to be executed in the right way. Children find it difficult to understand the mechanism of motion itself. Spinal muscles are not strong enough to hold the

**TABLE 6**

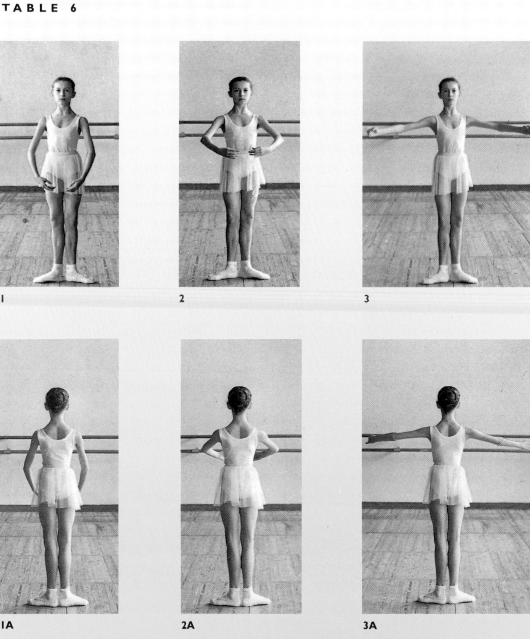

I                    2                    3

1A                  2A                  3A

arms in the correct position for a long time. For this reason it is advisable that the teacher should return to work on the positions periodically during the lesson rather than overload the pupils with tiring muscular training.

The goal of development artistry in children, in order to make their dance meaningful and spirited, must be set from the very first steps of the training. It is necessary to explain to the children what constitutes the beauty of arms put into a position and to substantiate the explanation with pictures of outstanding classical dancers. They should be told about the choreographic style with a special emphasis on the role that simple positions of arms play in the formation of that style, and on the poetry and meaning that are inherent in them. The air of old times in the romantic *La Sylphide* or *Giselle,* the impression of radiance and cheerfulness in *The Sleeping Beauty,* the slow melodious lyricism of the swan scenes in *The Swan Lake* – all of these are in a very large measure due to the arm positions which can be viewed as a major colour, a choreographic *leitmotif.* Demonstration by the teacher is of great importance for work on arms. The teacher must perfect the quality of demonstration and of his or her professional insight, and must be able to give accurate individual

4

4A

*Moscow 1980: Nina Ananlachvili in the ballet "La Fille Mal Gardée".*

**TABLE 7**

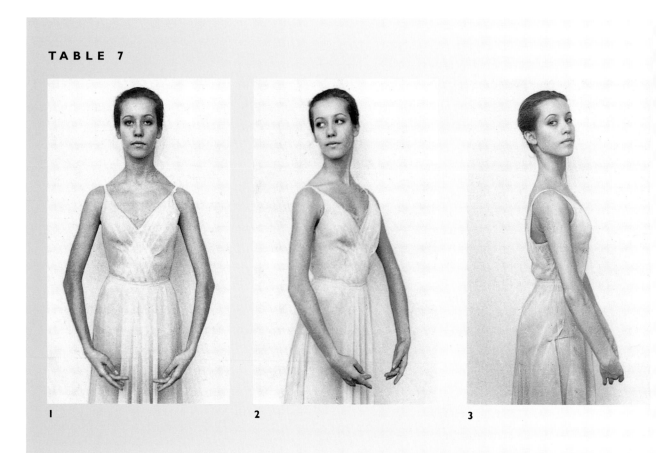

recommendations to the pupils in conformity with their individual constitutions.

The study of arm positions begins from the preparatory position. The preparatory position is oval-shaped. From the starting position (hands down on the sides, the feet in the half-turned-out 1st position), the arms are rounded a little at the elbows and fingers and take the shape of an oval, slightly in front of the body. They do not touch the body anywhere along their length, the palms are directed upwards and the fingers towards one another, with the hands at a distance of 2 or 3cm. The shoulders are thoroughly lowered and spread (*Table 7, photos 1-3*) and tend to a sloped shape merging with the preparatory position's oval. The neck line is straight but not strained. All the arm movements begin from the preparatory position. The lines of a correctly executed preparatory position should convey calm and dignity.

When explaining to the pupils what makes up the beauty of the preparatory position, the idea is to let them understand and feel the harmony and unity in the bearing of the head, neck and arms.

Initially, the execution of the preparatory position is controlled in the mirror, with the head in the *en face* position. When the pupils have mastered it, movements of the head and direction of the

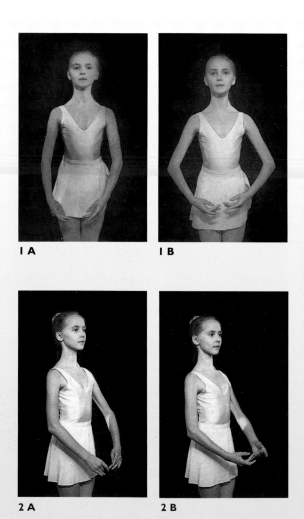

eyes are included in the position's build-up: the head is slightly lowered and the eyes are directed to the palms (the direction of the eyes is both a part of the position and a means to control the hand).

There is hardly any point in giving unequivocal recommendations about the distance between the hands and the body in the preparatory position, because that distance will depend on the arms' length and other bodily proportions. It is quite logical that none of the Soviet teacher's manuals specifies this detail.

There are, however, two extremes in suggesting the level to which the arms are raised in the preparatory position: some put it almost as high as the 1st position, while others place it very low with the fingers almost touching the body.

We believe that both these extremes are unnatural and affected. Some experienced teachers recommend that the hands should be held at about a palm's width from the body, the arms forming a long oval shape.

The following mistakes can be made when learning the preparatory position:

a) the arms are held too far in front of the body and nearly reach the 1st position, or, on the contrary, the hands almost touch the body;

b) the shoulders are not spread or lowered fully enough but are advanced forward and rounded;

c) the arms' upper part is pressed to the body as far as the elbows *(Table 7, photo 2b)*;

d) the arms are bent too much *(photo 1b)* or stretched out at the elbows too much *(photo 1a)*;

e) the hands are turned palms to the body *(photo 2a)* or are too wide apart.

The 1st position is the "gate" through which the arms can move into any other position or bearing. The arms, bended and rounded at the elbows and fingers, are a little higher than the waist with the palms facing the body *(Table 8, photos 1, 2)* and the hands almost touching each other. The visual effect of the 1st position is that it is more rounded than the preparatory or 3rd position. The figure's proportions in dance depend on the height at which the arms are held in the 1st position. It seems to divide the body into the upper and

**TABLE 8**

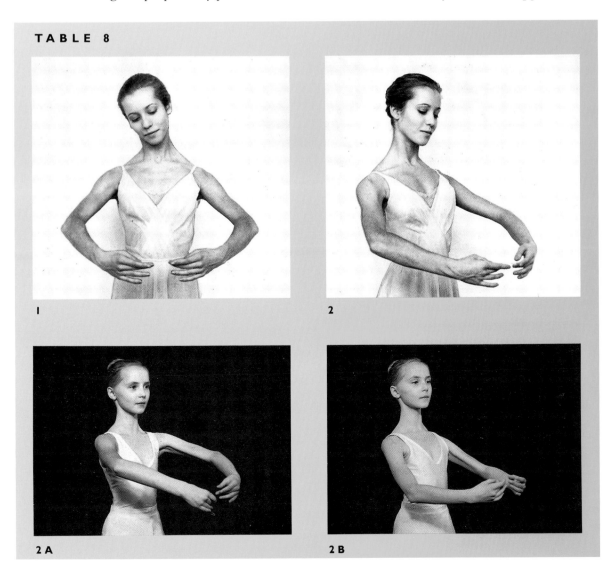

1 2

2 A 2 B

lower halves. A level too high or too low will distort the proportions and is therefore inadmissible.

The 1st position is an active help in leaps, rotations and movements on points and must be worked out thoroughly. If the arms are not rounded enough in the 1st position, they will not help in leaps and will interfere with rotations. At the same time the 1st position of arms should not be angular or lose smoothness.

The difficulty of the 1st position is that the muscular efforts of the arms and of the shoulder girdle are directed in opposite ways. To hold the arms correctly in the 1st and all other positions, it is necessary to have a good feeling of three points: the shoulder, elbow and hand joints. The shoulders must be lowered well enough, the elbows raised, and the hands, the elbow joint and the forearm should be held on one line.

In studying the 1st position the eyes should initially be directed toward the palms and the head should not be inclined. Later, at the teacher's suggestion, the head may be inclined slightly to the right or left shoulder and the eyes may look at either the right or left palm (photos 1, 2). N. I. Tarasov believes that this inclusion of head movements in the 1st position should most reasonably start at the bar when training the *préparation* (the opening of arms from the 1st position into the 2nd position).

The following mistakes can be made when learning the 1st position:

a) the shoulders are advanced forward to follow the arms, the circular shape is distorted (photo 2a) and is either too long (photo 2a) or too short (photo 2b);

b) the arms are held higher (photo 2a) or lower than appropriate;

c) the elbows are lowered while the forearm is raised (photo 2b), or, vice versa, the shoulders are raised while the forearms are lowered, and the hands are drooping (photo 2a).

The beauty of the 2nd position consists in its spread and smoothness.

The arms are mostly held in the 2nd position throughout any exercise session at the bar or in the middle. So it is the 2nd position that trains the strength of spinal, shoulder and forearm muscles more than any other, and it also helps keep the balance during exercises in the middle of the floor.

**TABLE 9**

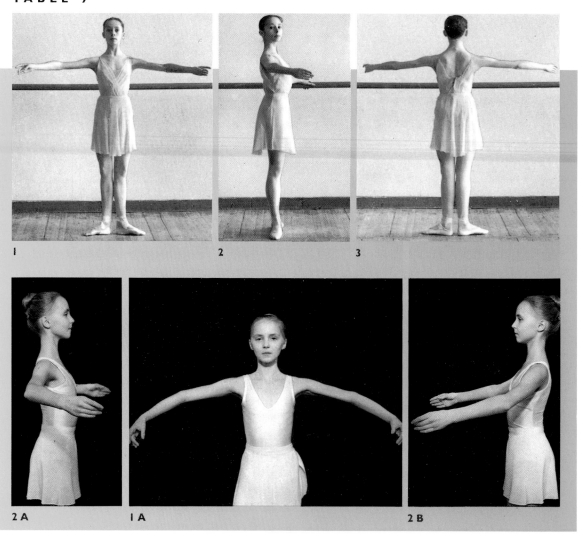

1
2
3

2A
1A
2B

TABLE 10

CARRIAGE OF THE HEAD 59

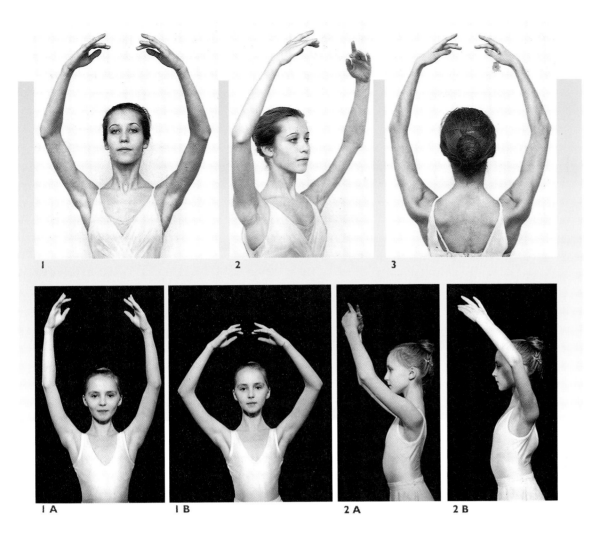

The arms are opened sideways a little below the shoulders and continue the shoulder line; they are slightly rounded at the elbow, and the shoulders are well spread. The hand, the forearm and the elbow joint are on the same horizontal line (*Table 9, photos 1-3*). In junior classes it is admissible for the arms in the 2nd position to be rounded to a greater extent, which helps develop balance in the middle of the floor.

In male classes, the arms can be opened a little wider from the elbows and their upper part must be upheld in a more active manner, which gives the position's outline a nuance of strong will.

A number of mistakes can be made when learning the 2nd position:

a) the elbows sag; the shoulders are raised while the forearms is lowered and is not on the same horizontal line with the shoulder (*Table 9, photo 1a*);

b) the arms are too outstretched at elbows;

c) the elbows are either behind the shoulder line (*photo 2a*) or too far in front of the shoulders (*photo 2b*).

The 3rd position has an upward tendency, it crowns the performer's figure and gives a smooth circular frame to his or her head and neck.

The 3rd position is similar in shape to the preparatory position. It is a kind of raised preparatory position. The arms with rounded elbows, which are set aide, are raised into an oval shape a little in front of the body; they must be visible to the pupil without raising his or her head; and the hands are closed to a distance of 2 or 3cm between the fingers (*Table 10, photos 1-3*).

Very strong spinal muscles are needed to hold the arms in the 3rd position correctly, as the shoulders are strongly lowered while the arms are up. It takes some very active work by the shoulder muscle to hold the arms in the correct position.

Initially, the position's correct shape is controlled with the help of the mirror. Later the head and the eyes are included in the position's setup.

From the *en face* position, the head is raised high enough to see the hands. Later, while keeping the arms in the 3rd position, the head can be raised from the *en face* position with a slight turn left and an inclination to the left shoulder; the eyes may look at the right palm or elsewhere.

**TABLE 10**

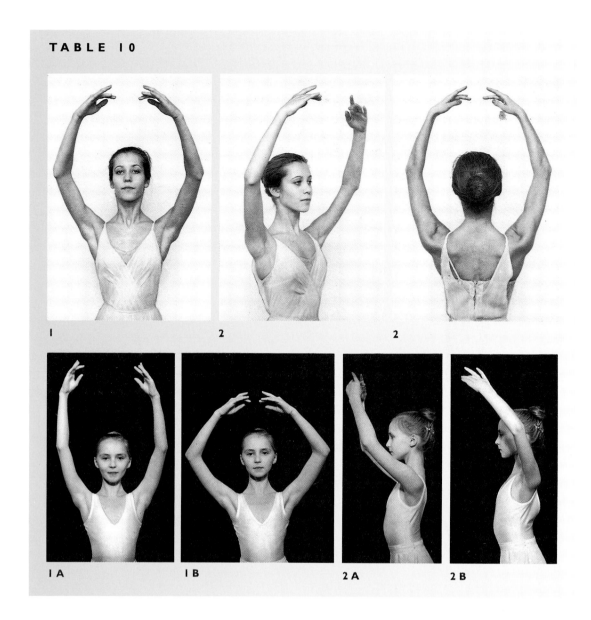

Head turns are inclinations in the 3rd position and can be varied: the chin may be lowered as you look under the arm, or the head may be turned into a profile etc. This is preparation for the head and the eyes to take part in the port de bras.

A number of mistakes may appear when learning the 3rd position:

a) the shoulders are raised to follow the arms (*Table 10, photo 1a*);

b) the arms are raised higher *(photo 1a)* or lower than appropriate *(photo 1b)*;

c) the elbows and shoulders are directed forward *(photo 2a)* or drawn back *(photo 2b)*;

d) the arms are too bent at the elbows *(photo 1b)* or too elongated *(photo 1a)*;

e) the hands are drooping down with the palms turned outwards *(photo 2b)*.

The arms go from one position to another by being raised, lowered, opened or closed. This is the reason why the study of the positions should be accompanied by work on the basic elements of the *port de bras:* the raising, lowering, opening and closing of arms.

*Louzina in the ballet "Coppélia".*

*The ballet "Giselle". The Odessa Opera and Ballet Company.*

# Basic elements of Port de Bras

*Port de bras* literally means "carriage of the arms". The goal of learning this movement is the ability to maintain the arms' correct shape when raising, lowering, opening, closing or otherwise transferring them from one position to another. The *port de bras* is a kind of ligature between one position or pose and another. The movement should therefore be executed smoothly .

The *port de bras* is based on the laws of harmony and expedience.

This movement seeks in the first place to find the shortest and most logical path for the arms to travel when changing a position or pose. The *port de bras* organizes the dance and makes it upright and well defined. The arms' two basic functions in the *port de bras* are those of decoration and assistance in dance; these have been pointed out by all outstanding ballet teachers from Carlo Blasis and Jean-Georges Noverre to A. Vaganova and N. Tarasov.

"If the arms follow the body's movements precisely, they can be compared to a frame round a picture. If the frame doesn't match the picture, the painting will lose in quality no matter how good it is. The same is true of a dancer: no matter how graceful he is in executing his steps, he will never attain real appeal or true grace if his arms are inflexible and are not in full harmony with the legs,"[1] Carlo Blasis wrote.

"… it is only if the dancer finds the right place for her arms that her artistic image will be complete and there will be full harmony in her dance,"[2] maintained Vaganova two hundred years later.

The basic elements of the port de bras add strength, flexibility, and expressiveness to the upper part of the trunk, the shoulders, arms and hands.

They serve as an instrument to streamline the arms' movement from one position to another and to work out the fundamental laws of classical dance arm motion: the arms being "separate" from the body and coordinated with the movements of the body and head. Correct execution of *port de bras* elements demands attention to the beauty, dignity and expressiveness of any gesture. This is why maximum effort should be made to make their execution expressive, smooth and unbroken.

A higher level of work on arms in the *port de bras* includes head motion and involvement of the eyes to convey meaning,

1. Quoted from: *Klassiki Khoreografii* (Classical Teachers of Choreography). Moscow-Leningrad, 1937, p. 111.

2. A. Ya. Vaganova. *Osnovy Klassicheskogo Tantsa* (Fundamentals of Classical Dance), p. 56.

expression and artistry to the movements of the arms. It is from this moment on that the pupil must become aware of such concepts as the character of movement and the multiple variety of its nuances. For example, when explaining the rules of performing the elementary *port de bras* it is necessary to stress that the opening of the arms into the 1st and 2nd positions must be wide, the "sigh" must be light and gentle, and the lowering of the arms must be smooth and calm.

Every teacher will find their own imaginative or emotional prompts to develop expressive and artistic execution of the *port de bras* in his or her pupils, in line with the nature of the music, the pupil's age and the teacher's own understanding of the ideal movement.

As the governing principle of classical dance teaching methods requires progress from the simple to the more complex, the recommended sequence of the positions to study is one which permits work on the arms' transfer from one position to another by stages in ever-increasing degrees of difficulty.

---

Positions are studied in the following order: preparatory, 1st, 2nd and 3rd. The study of rounded positions (all except the 2nd one) should be accompanied by the simultaneous raising of the arms. Work on these positions is concluded by mastering the 1st preparatory form of the *port de bras:* raising of arms from the preparatory position into the 1st position and then lowering into the 3rd position. The goal of this simplest form of the port de bras is that the circular shape be preserved while moving the arms up and down (Table 11, photos a→b→c←b←a). The arms move symmetrically and simultaneously in this form of the *port de bras*.

When explaining this *port de bras* form, the pupils' attention should be called to the basic elements found in all other forms (raising and lowering). The raising and lowering should be watched for well-spread and lowered shoulders and shoulder blades.

The study of the *port de bras* begins in the *en face* position (allowing for visual mirror control) with the feet half turned out,

and each position should be fixated for a long time.

N. I. Tarasov recommends that eyes should be involved in these simpler forms of the *port de bras* first at the bar and then in the middle of the floor. When at the bar, it is logical to start developing a sense of the central vertical line along which the arm is raised or lowered. This element will later be encountered in the middle-of-the-floor *port de bras* with alternate movements of the arms.

When working at this *port de bras,* special attention should be paid to the raising of arms from the 1st to the 3rd position and their lowering from the 3rd into the 1st position. During the lifting movement, the shoulders and shoulder blades act as the muscular counterpoise (arms up – shoulders down). The arms are lowered from the 3rd position into the preparatory position with well spread and lowered shoulders in a fixated state. The elbows are held slightly aside during the raising movement.

**A 1**

**B 1**

**C 1**

**A 2**

TABLE II

CARRIAGE OF THE HEAD **63**

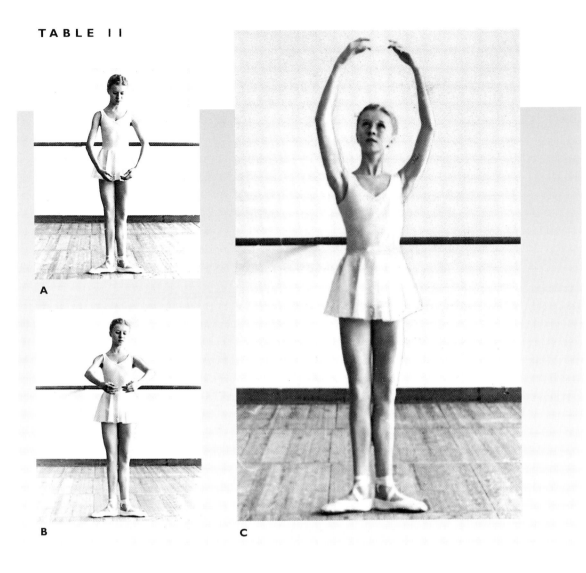

A

B

C

This form of the *port de bras* strengthens muscles in the upper part of the arm and spine and helps train the "separateness" of the arms from the body in motion. As junior class teaching experience has shown, it is this "separateness" that the pupils find very hard to master at first. The shoulders most often disobey the pupil and either move forward or go up together with the arms.

To help a student feel that his or her arms are independent from the body and develop the appropriate muscular feeling, the following device is recommendable: the teacher puts his or her hands on the student's shoulders and helps fixate the lowered shoulders during the movement by pressing them down lightly and preventing them from following the arms *(Table 11, photo a(1), b(1), c(1))*.

The teacher can also help the student feel the correct arm shape during the lift

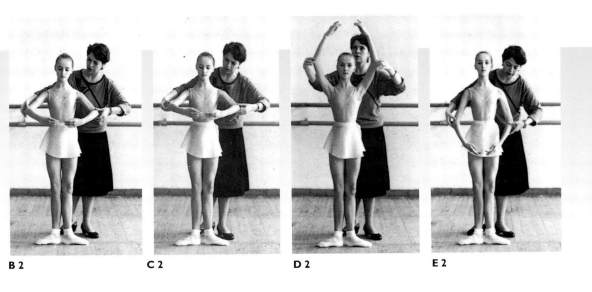

B 2

C 2

D 2

E 2

TABLE 12

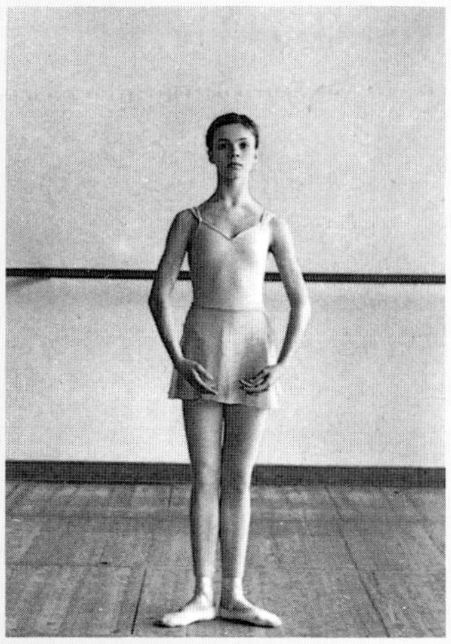

A

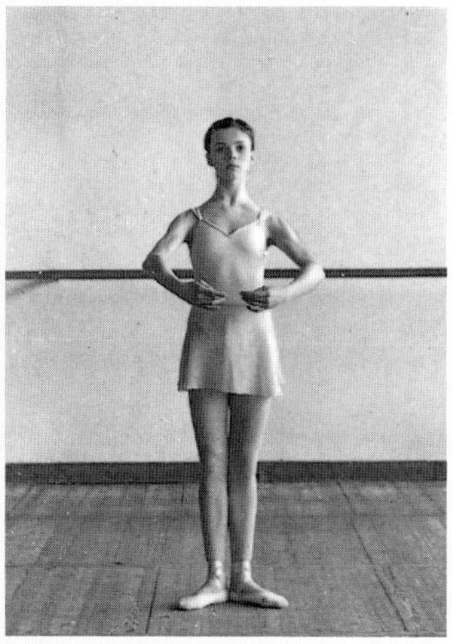

B

C

D

E

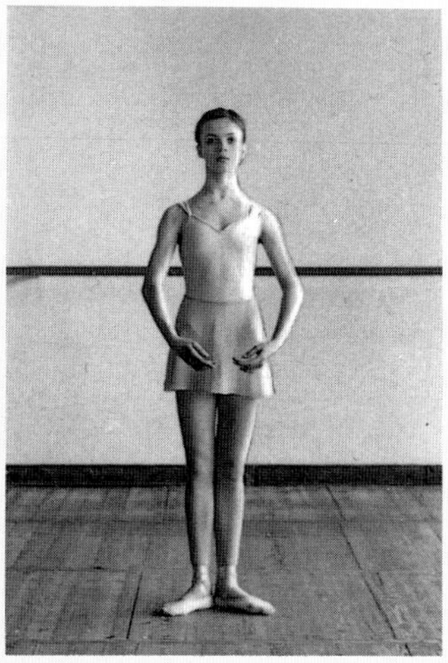

F

A1

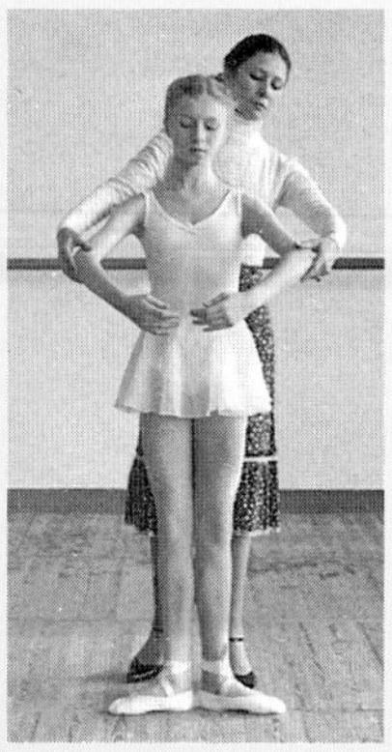

B1

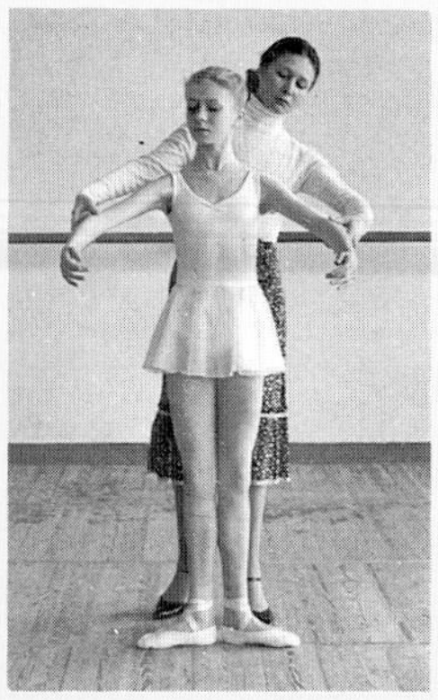

C1

D1

E1

F1

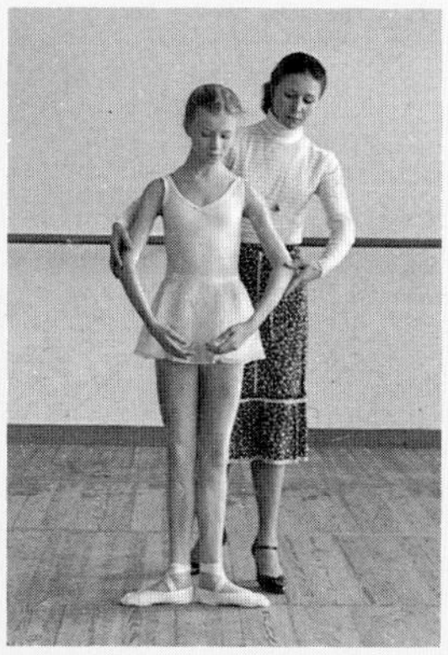

G1

phase by supporting his or her elbows and slightly moving them aside as the arms go into the 3rd position *(photo a(2), b(2), c(2), d(2), e(2))*.

When the technical skill has been mastered, a slight raising and slanting movement of the head is added, incorporating the involvement of the eyes. The eyes are looking at the palms and watch them in motion. The head may be held with a right or left inclination, according to the teacher's assignment.

The next form of the *port de bras*

involves the lifting of arms from the preparatory into the 1st position, followed by opening them into the 2nd position and lowering them into the preparatory position *(Table 12, photos a, b, c, d, e, f)*. The opening of arms from the 1st into the 2nd position starts from the hand, with their upper part fixed. It is not until the forearm is opened to elbow level and the intermediate is reached between the 1st and 2nd positions that the whole arm is included in the movement and brought into the 2nd position.

**TABLE 13**

A  B  C

*M. Plisetskaya and N. Fadieitchev in "The Sleeping Beauty".*

D  E  F

A1  B1  C1  D1  E1  F1  G1

The following device is recommended to let the pupil understand the technique of performing this phase of the movement: the teacher supports the pupil's elbows *(photo b(1))* until the lower part of the arm (from the hand to the elbow) is opened to elbow level *(photo b(1))*, and only then helps bring the arms to the 2nd position.

The next point to be made in teaching this form of the *port de bras* is the so-called "hand sigh" before the arms are lowered, plus the lowering as such. The "sigh" begins with the opening of fingers and the transfer of the palm into the *allongé* position facing down. It should be watched that the wrist does not bend out, that the fingers are elongated and not tense as they open, and that the turn itself is done in an economical movement *(photos d(1), e(1))*. The arms should be supported in the upper part, so that they are lowered as if from the shoulder blades. The finger tips lag behind a little.

When arms are lowered and have covered three-quarters of the way, they are in the *allongé* position *(photos e(1) → f(1))*. After that, while the upper part of the arm remains fixed, they are rounded from the elbows and closed into an arrondi in the preparatory position *(photos f(1) → g(1))*. The closing is completed by the fingers.

The following device is recommendable in order to help the pupil feel the forearm's independence of the upper part of the hand during closure: the teacher supports the pupil's elbows *(photos e(1), f(1))* and helps lower the arms to point e(1), following which only the hand and the forearm are involved in the movement; he fixates the upper part of the arm to immobility at the point of their closure into the preparatory position *(photos f(1) → g(1))*.

When this form of the *port de bras* has been technically mastered, head bends and turns are added as well as the eyes. When the arms are raised from the preparatory position into the 1st position, the eyes may look at the right (or left) palm and the head may be slightly inclined toward the left (or right) shoulder. When the arms are opened, the head turns to follow the right (or left) hand and after the "sigh" an inclined head and the eyes follow the lowering of the right (or left) arm.

The next preparatory form of the *port de bras* involves the lifting of arms from the preparatory position through the 1st into the 3rd position, then opening them into the 2nd position and lowering into the preparatory position *(Table 13, photos a, b, c, d, e, f)*. A new element – the opening of arms from the 3rd into the 2nd position – is included in this form of the *port de bras*. It may require special attention to train.

This element of movement has two phases: phase 1 involves the hand and the forearm, and phase 2, the whole arm.

To train this element it may be necessary (especially at the beginning) to fixate the intermediate state between the 3rd and 2nd positions *(photo d(1))*. The following device is recommended in this case: the teacher supports the pupil's elbows until the forearm is opened to elbow level *(photos b(1) → d(1))*, then, while supporting the elbows still, the teacher helps put the arms into the 2nd position as the hands turn slowly and assume a stance natural for the 2nd position.

After the pupils learn to open their arms from the 3rd into the 2nd position, head movements and the eyes are included in the exercise. The eyes should follow the movements of either the right or the left hand *(photos a(1), b(1), c(1), d(1), e(1), f(1), g(1))*.

**TABLE 14**

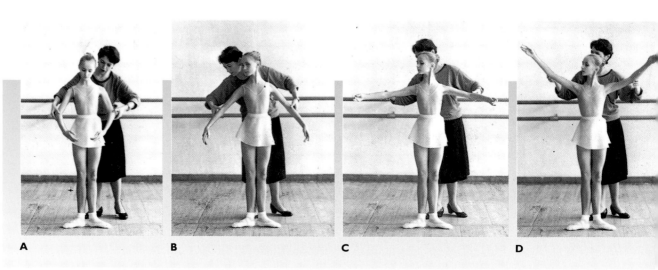

A     B     C     D

*"Swan Lake". The Kirov Company.*

The preparatory forms of the *port de bras* allow the training of the arms' reverse movement *(en dedans)*. Pure *en dedans* is not as frequent as *en dehors* in classical dance, but its elements are present in a number of the basic *port de bras* forms.

It is recommended that the study of the *port de bras* with *en dedans* movement should begin with forms where the arms work simultaneously and symmetrically.

The following form can be suggested for initial training: from the preparatory position the arms are lifted into the 2nd position, then the 3rd position, whence they are lowered into the preparatory position through the 1st position *(Table 14, photos a, b, c, d, e, f, g)*. Ye. P. Gerdt used to

include this *port de bras* in her lessons as a compulsory exercise.

The first part of the movement is executed with the fixed upper part of the arm (from the shoulder joint to the elbow). The movement should seem to begin from the nails *(photo a → b)*, the fingers lag behind slightly, and when it is halfway between the preparatory and 2nd positions the whole arm is included in the movement; the hands and the forearm turn slowly to gain their natural setting in the 2nd position *(photos b → c)*.

The raising of arms from the 2nd to the 3rd position also consists of two phases: phase 1 involves the whole arm *(photos c → d)*, and when it is halfway between the preparatory and 2nd positions the hand and forearm complete the movement *(photos d → e)*.

In order that the hands do not turn palm outwards during the arm lift from the 2nd to the 3rd position, they must be turned gradually into what is natural for them in the 3rd position. If the hand turns into the 3rd position too early the movement loses its naturalness and becomes affected. If, on the contrary, the hand remains too long with its palm outward it acquires excessive mannerism and the "litter" of an extra turn of the hand.

It is advisable that this form of the *port de bras* be trained initially in the *en face* position with mirror control. The next step

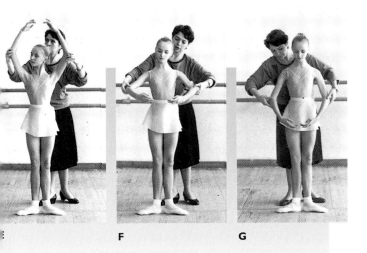

F            G

*E. Maximova in the ballet "Icarus".*

**TABLE 15**

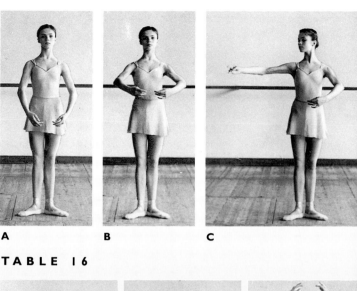

A           B           C

**TABLE 16**

A           B           C

in mastering the movement involves the inclusion of head bends and turns with eye participation.

The next-in-turn variety of the *port de bras* helps train the alternate movements of arms covering identical paths. Alternate arm motion versions of the *port de bras* can be varied, but head movements and the eyes should be included in the practice from the very beginning.

After the arms are lifted from the preparatory to the 1st and then 2nd position, first the right hand and then the left hand are opened *(Table 15, photos a, b, c, d, e, f, g)*. The opening of each hand into the 2nd position is accompanied by the respective turn of the head and the eyes.

A similar version of the *port de bras* can be worked out with the 3rd position included: first the right and then left hand will be opened from the 3rd into 2nd position *(Table 16, photos a, b, c, d, e, f, g)*.

Given here is one of the preparatory forms of the *port de bras* (including both symmetrical/simultaneous and alternate arm motion) which Ye. P. Gerdt recommended as a preparation for the study of major and minor poses.

The movement is executed *en face* in the 1st position of feet. After the arms are lifted from the preparatory position first into the 1st and then 3rd position (eyes watching the hands), the left arm is lowered into the 1st position (eyes watching the left palm with the head slightly inclined to the right), following which it is opened into the 2nd position (eyes following the arm's

**TABLE 17**

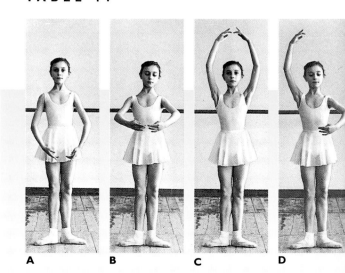

A           B           C           D

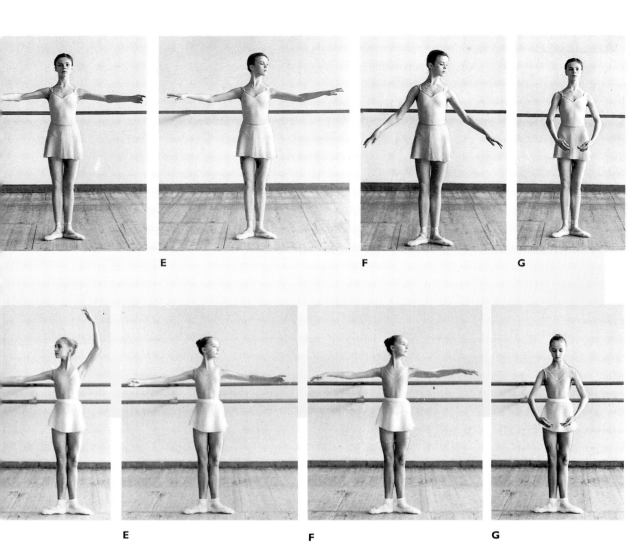

E                F                G

E                F                G

movement); then the right arm goes the same way. At the end the arms are lowered into the preparatory position *(Table 17, photos a, b, c, d, e, f, g, h)*.

When performing this *port de bras* form it is helpful to fixate the state when one arm is in the 1st position, the other in the 3rd position *(photo f)*; or one arm in the 3rd position, the other in the 2nd position *(photo e)*. The arm which is in either the 1st or 3rd position *(photo d)* should be watched not to cross the imaginary vertical line dividing the performer's figure in two, nor to depart from it. Concentrated work on this stance helps retain the precision of pose patterns.

Among other elements of the *port de bras* that should be studied together with

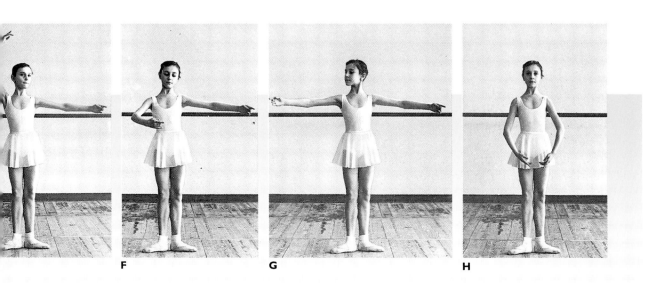

F                G                H

the positions it is good to work in a slow tempo on an arm movement which is amply employed in leaps, point dance and rotations: the so-called "catch-up" of the arms.

Arms in the "catch-up" are opened a little from the preparatory position sideways (the opening starts from finger tips) and then closed again into the preparatory position *(Table 18, photos a, b, c)*. The arm position as they are opened sideways to elbow level halfway between the preparatory and 2nd position is called *demi-second* (half-2nd position) by some authors *(photos b, b(1))*.

To help a pupil develop a muscular feeling of the forearm's independence of the upper arm, the following device could be helpful: the teacher, who is standing behind the pupil, supports his or her elbows and fixates them in the open position while the pupil opens his or her arms to elbow level or from the 1st position into a stance halfway between the 1st and 2nd positions, and then closes them back *(photos a(1), b(1), c(1))*.

When this movement is executed as "catch-up" later, the concept of emphasis should be introduced in order to ensure its appropriate execution. The arms are opened in order to raise them from the preparatory position *(photo b)* into the 1st position *(photo a(a))*, so the emphasis in the movement should be made on the arm lift (the preparatory position in this case is a passing one on the way to the 1st position).

Elements of the *port de bras* learned together with the positions will later be incorporated in all the arm movements and major *port de bras* forms, and be executed according to the same rules.

**TABLE 18**

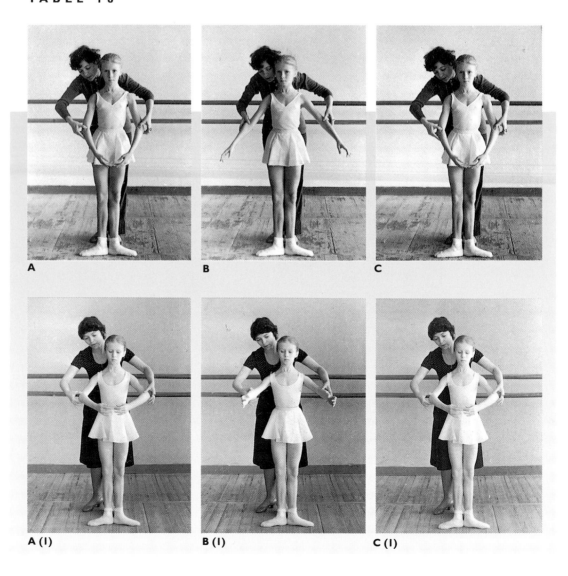

A     B     C

A (1)    B (1)    C (1)

*Maya Plisetskaya in "The Sleeping Beauty".*

## Poses

The study of arm positions and the basic elements of the *port de bras* leads the pupils to the next and higher stage of work on arms: the study of poses.

The pose is the key symbol of the language of dance. True classical dance consists of poses connected by movements.

A pose consists of a certain combination of arm positions, positions of the feet and body, an inclination or turn of the head, and the direction of the performer's eyes with respect to the spectator. These combinations were once defined so precisely and aptly that they became capable of giving birth to dance, just like music is born of a few notes.

The character of a pose and its emotional and visual form are determined by the graphical pattern formed by the arms, legs, body and head.

There are only a few poses: *croisé* (forward and backward), *effacé* (forward and backward), *écarté* (forward and backward), *arabesque* (first, second, third and fourth) and attitude (*croisé and effacé*). They differ in pattern, orientation and character. Their names reflect, to a certain extent, the poses' imagery and setup. At the same time, each pose has vast capabilities of variation within the range of its special imaginative and formal features.

Said N. I. Tarasov: "The power and emotional strength of every pose in dance do not emerge from a leg raised 90 degrees or higher, but from the student's ability to comprehend the choreographic structure and character of performance."[1]

Discoveries in ballet were made by those choreographers and performers who were able to sense the pose's exact visual intonation inherent in its graphical pattern.

As an example, the self-styled pattern of the second *arabesque* gave an impetus to the fantasy of Filippo Taglioni, the 19th-century early romantic choreographer, (and later also to Auguste Bournonville and Michel Fokine) in finding a visual *leitmotif* for the heroine of the ballet *La Sylphide.* That pose's design was a very apt characteristic for a light, subtle and capricious creature ready to escape.

A pose is coloured by the choreographer's fantasy on the one hand and the performer's personality on the other.

1. N.I. Tarasov. *Klassicheskiy Tanets* (Classical Dance). Moscow, 1971, p. 185.

The highest examples of scenic art are a cross between the discoveries of the choreographer who has aptly revealed the pose's emotional and imaginative essence, and its interpretation by the equally inspired performer. The performer in that case is not only a subtle interpreter but also a co-author of the choreographer. The pose then continues to develop in time and to live a life of its own, becoming independent of its creators as a symbol of beauty.

The fleeting and unsteady design of the *arabesque* by Pavlova as the Sylphide (depicted by Valentin Serov in a placard issued for the beginning of the Russian Seasons in Paris at the beginning of this century) became a symbol and embodiment of Russian ballet: "a flight full of soul."

The proud bearing of Semenova's *attitude* is inseparable in the minds of several generations of Soviet ballet spectators from the young princess Aurora in Petipa's choreographic masterpiece created in a long past era.

A pose is the first graphic manifestation of artistry and the first tool to disclose the performer's personality, immature as it may be. Bearing that in mind, the teacher should be very tactful and careful about pose training; while trying to develop the pupil's taste and correctness in execution, he or she should not attempt to suppress the first glimpses of individuality.

"Various deviations are possible from the above canonical poses in scenic dance, unless they distort their essence. However, in studying the poses it is necessary that the canonical forms and all their constituent details should be mastered. One should not even be afraid of some dryness or schematicism. There is no need to press for expressiveness in junior classes as it may lead to mannerisms,"[1] wrote N. I. Tarasov.

Although the constructive basis of the pose is invariable, its design and character will change in the intermediate and senior classes by becoming more impressively graphical. The scholarly pattern as it appears initially is going to become more individualized. For example, a sideways-opened arm in the *arabesque* is held strictly against the shoulder in junior classes, but in intermediate and especially senior classes it can be drawn back "as far as the normal position of the shoulder permits,"[2] which adds width and span to the *arabesque*.

The backward *écarté* pose can only acquire finished design after there has been sufficient setup training for the back – i.e. in the 4th year.

Still, pupils must be taught to feel the character of the pose at an early stage of training.

Ye. P. Gerdt is known to have attached great significance to the development of artistry when working on poses at all stages of training. The results of her work with students as well as the methodological and photographic materials of the Moscow Ballet School Teaching Methods Division (Bulletin 1958/59, No.2 and 3, pp.57-58) testify to a great qualitative breakthrough in pose work in middle and senior classes. The upper part of the body is more actively involved in movement, the hollow under the shoulder blades is deeper, the turn of the head is more expressive, and there appears a great number of variations and nuances in body and head movements. This plentitude of pose variations which the

**1.** V. Moritz, N. Tarasov, A. Chekrygin. *Metodika Klassicheskogo Trenazha* (Classical Dance Teaching Methods), p. 57.
**2.** Ibid., p. 53.

**L. Semeniaka and M. Liepa in "Giselle".**

teacher introduced in the exercises with so much artistic freedom, and also the subtlety and variety of nuances and shades, all serve to foster artistry and naturalness in students and to make them true performers.

In intermediate and particularly senior classes the pose penetrates into almost all parts of the lesson, including *allegro,* rotations and points. Pose fixation at the top point of a leap creates the effect of prolonged flight and the impression of the body resting in air. The graphicness of a pose is the form-organizing factor; it adds span to rotations in major poses.

Finally, the pose triumphs in scenic creations. Its intonational structure is what brings forth a choreographic style.

Work on the pose begins with the *épaulement* position. The turning of the figure from the *en face* to the *épaulement* position signifies a new stage in training. It is together with the *épaulement* that the students should learn the concept of "light and shade": the *épaulement* helps them to go over from the flat, straightforward design to three-dimensional movement. When the performer's figure is viewed by the spectator in semi-profile, the proportions of the shoulder angle, the hips and the working leg with regard to a certain point create the interplay of lines in the overall design of the pose.

When starting to work on a pose, it is necessary to explain to the students the significance of the *épaulement* in its build-up and the need for its precise execution.

Understandably enough, the most widespread mistakes associated with pose training are those which are due to the insufficiently well-trained *épaulement*.

"The execution of the *épaulement* demands exactness and plastic aplomb from the trainee. Any lack of precision or assurance in the bearing of the shoulders, the turn of the head or the direction of the eyes must be ruled out."[1]

**1.** N.I. Tarasov. *Klassicheskiy Tanets* (Classical Dance). Moscow, 1971, p. 166.

TABLE 19

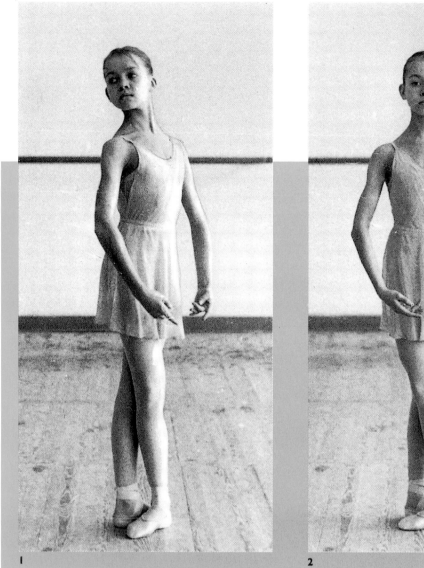

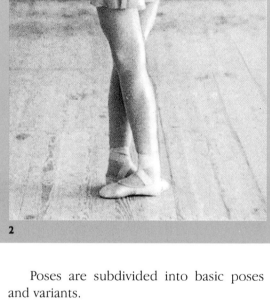

1

2

All the poses are built on two stances: *épaulement croisé (Table 19, photo 1)* and *effacé (photo 3)*. These should be worked out thoroughly before learning the poses.

In *épaulement croisé* the shoulders and hips are spread along the diagonal line connecting pt.6 and pt.2; the body is directed towards pt.8. The foot corresponding to the shoulder turned towards the mirror is in position V in front. The head is also turned to the mirror.

In *épaulement effacé* the shoulder and hips are in the same diagonal as in *croisé,* but it is the foot opposite the shoulder turned towards the mirror that is in position V in front. The head is also turned to the mirror.

To develop a better sense of the pose's spatial design, it is recommended to work on it first in the middle of the floor, and then at the bar. Poses are classified as major and minor. They differ in character and emotional colouring. The major poses are executed with the compulsory inclusion of the 3rd position.

Poses are subdivided into basic poses and variants.

When considering the graphical composition and spatial orientation of a pose N. I. Tarasov gives a chart of the poses' constructive elements in his textbook (see drawings of the poses in the book *Classical Dance*). He stresses the fundamental significance of the two intersecting lines of the support and working legs with regard to the floor plane.

A pose, however, does not only have volume, but also height. It seems to grow up, so we find it necessary to add to N. I. Tarasov's description the vertical core of the poses, made up of the support leg line, the trunk and the arm raised into the 3rd position.

For the pose design to be more graphical, it is necessary to observe the precise directions of the working leg and the support leg as underscored by the N. I. Tarasov scheme (see N. I. Tarasov's book *Classical Dance,* section *Poses*), and also to

3

As soon as they are learned, the major and minor poses are included in the exercise at the bar in the group of *adagio*, rotations, toe dance and jumps.

For better precision of the leg pattern in the poses it is recommended that different variations are worked from arm combinations in the *en face* position with the feet in position I, and then in the *épaulement* with the feet in positions I and V *(Table 19, photo 1(1), 1(2), 3(1) and 3(2))*. This helps the student feel the imaginary vertical line dividing the performer's figure in half, which the arm in the 3rd or 1st position must not cross or depart from.

In the first year the major poses are executed with the toes on the floor, in the second year, with leg raised 90 degrees and the other foot resting on the floor, and in the third year on half-toes. Initially it is recommended, while standing in the 5th position, first to open the arms into a pose and then to stretch out the leg. The next stage involves a more collective execution: while standing in the 5th position, the arms should be lifted into the 1st position and then opened into a pose with the leg set out simultaneously. At the point when the arms are opened from the 1st position into the *arabesque* the hands should be watched to turned palm down without bending at the wrist. *Arabesque* poses end in returning to the initial position when the arms are

1(2)  1(1)  3(1)  3(2)

observe the unity and purity of the line that constitutes the pose's vertical core.

The minor poses are similar to the major poses, but their arm design is based on the combination of the 1st and 2nd positions. First the major poses are studied in the middle of the floor, and then the minor poses.

lowered, retaining the *arabesque's* characteristic *allongé* outline for three-quarters of their way, following which they are gradually rounded.

Beginning from the third year, variants of the poses are studied. The design, character and colouring of a pose will be

**TABLE 20**

1

2

2 A

2 B

changed by such details as the height to which the arms are raised, the position of the hand, a body or head bend or turn, and the direction of the eyes. It is the nuances that give a pose a certain expression or character.

Changing a pose for a variant (with the invariable *épaulement*) is done through a number of techniques:

a) change in the arm position;

b) changes in the positions of the body or head or in the direction of the eyes;

c) a number of poses can be executed with arms in the 3rd position, and also in the *allongé* position;

d) in all the poses the 2nd-position arm can be transferred to the 1st position;

e) the *arabesque* can be changed by transferring the opened 2nd-position arm into the 1st position with an *allongé* hand.

In middle and senior classes work is continued not only on the techniques of performing *adagios*, jumps and rotations, but also on the further improvement of the gestures and the stylistic and artistic colouring of the pose. Advancement of artistry in the intermediate and senior classes is associated with qualitative

I (1)

I (2)

I (3)

**1.** *Bulleten Metodkabineta MAKhU* (Bulletin of MAKhU Teaching Methods Division), No. 1. Moscow, 1958/59. p.54

*G. Oulanova in "The Fountain of Bakhchisaray".*

**2 C**          **2 D**

poses must be the *épaulement croisé* as a rule. More complicated *effacé* and *écarté* poses are first studied from the *épaulement effacé* and then *épaulement croisé* positions.

The *croisé* pose is based on the intersecting lines of the working and support legs. The support (left) leg, the shoulders and hips are spread along the diagonal line connecting pt.6 and pt.2; the working (right) leg is stretched out forward to toe *(Table 20, photo 1)* or raised 90 degrees *(photo 2)* in the direction between pt.8 and pt.1. The (left) arm corresponding to the support leg is raised into the 3rd position, and the (right) arm corresponding to the leg opened to toe is in the 2nd position. The head is turned toward the 2nd-position arm, the eyes looking the same way.

Variants of the forward *croisé* are given in photos 2a, 2b, 2c, 2d.

Mistakes made in the study of the *croisé* are mostly due to an imprecise *épaulement*. This imprecision is associated with the wrong hip line and a shift of the diagonal in which the performer's figure should be positioned with regard to a certain point. As a result, the 2nd-position arm goes forward together with the shoulder *(Table 20, photo 1(2))*, or backward *(photo 1(1))*, or crosses that diagonal *(photo 1(3))*. The 3rd-position arm's elbow is sometimes directed forward *(photo 1(3))*. All this impairs the graphical precision of the pose.

With the possibility of such mistakes in view, it is necessary to watch the accuracy of the *épaulement* and the arm position. The arm raised into the 3rd position should be watched so as not to depart sideways from the central vertical line dividing the figure nor to cross that line. The elbow must be well opened, the shoulder joint lowered, and the elbow of the 2nd-position arm should be actively supported.

The backward *croisé* pose has a similar basis to the forward *croisé*, retaining the same body turn, arm position and head turn. What is different is the direction of the leg stretched to toe or raised, and therefore the relationship between the arm and foot positions. The arm opened into the 2nd position corresponds to the support (right) leg, while the arm raised into the 3rd position, to the left leg opened backward into pt.4. The head is turned to face the arm opened into the 2nd position. The trunk is upright to give the

changes in the work on the pose, seeking the development of a flexible and expressive upper trunk, a smooth neck line, sloping shoulders and an inspired directional glance. "If the eyes are slanting into the mirror, the pose will inevitably look false,"[1] wrote Ye. P. Gerdt.

The following sequence is recommended in the study of poses.

The early stage should involve the forward and backward *croisé*, then the forward and backward *effacé*, and then the forward and backward *écarté*. Following that, the four arabesques should be studied. The initial position for the study of the

TABLE 21

pose a stable and assured character *(Table 21, photos 1, 2)*.

Variants of the backward *croisé* are given in *photos 2a, 2b, 2c, 2d.*

Mistakes made in the study of this *croisé* are also due to an imprecise *épaulement* as well as to the bearings and lines of the arms in the 2nd and 3rd positions. Also, the side of the working leg is often clamped, the support hip may sink, causing the shoulders and arms to lose evenness and the pose its graphicness.*(photos 1(1), 1(2), 1(3)).*

The design and character of the *effacé* are softer than in the *croisé* and are marked

1

2 A

2 B

2 C

2 D

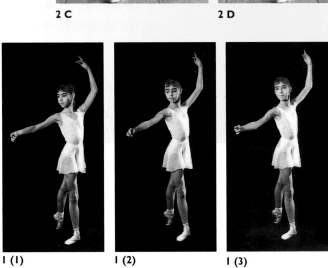

1 (1)          1 (2)          1 (3)

2

by a more active involvement of the upper trunk, shoulder and head.

The *effacé,* just like the *épaulement effacé,* gives an emphasis to the open and widespread position of the figure. The arm corresponding to the support leg is raised into the 3rd position, the shoulders are a little back, the head is turned toward the arms raised into the 3rd position and slightly back, too, and the eyes are looking slightly above the elbow.

The arm corresponding to the leg stretched to toe or raised 90 degrees is opened into the 2nd position. The support leg, the body and the 3rd-position arm form the core of the pose *(Table 22, photos 1, 2).*

Variants of the forward *effacé* are given in *photos 2a, 2b, 2c, 2d.*

Mistakes made in the execution of the *effacé* are due to an imprecise *épaulement.*

The more distant half of the body (with regard to the spectator) is not drawn back fully enough; the 2nd-position arm is misplaced and comes forward together with the shoulder; thus the purity of shoulder and arm lines and the pose's graphicness are impaired *(photo 1(3)).* The arm raised into the 3rd position departs from the

**TABLE 22**

I                  2

2 A       I A       I A       I A

I (1)       I (2)       I (3)

**TABLE 23**

| I | I |
| --- | --- |

| 2 A | 2 B | 2 C | 2 D |

central axis *(photo 1(3))*, the shoulders are not drawn back well enough *(photos 1(1), 1(2), 1(3))*, the head turn is not distinct enough *(photos 1(1), 1(2))* and the pose is slurred. The shoulder of the 3rd-position arm is lifted.

The backward *effacé* pose is forward-directed and flying. The arm corresponding to the leg stretched to toe or raised 90 degrees is lifted to the 3rd position, while the arm corresponding to the support leg is in the 2nd position. The body is drawn a little forward, the head is slightly bent toward the arm opened into the 2nd position, the eyes are looking into the distance past the wrist, but not "under the arm" *(Table 23, photos 2, 3)*. It should be watched that the whole support side is held actively without turning toward the working side. The arm raised into the 3rd position should hold the centre, the elbow must be well opened, and the hand of the 2nd-position arm should be actively supported.

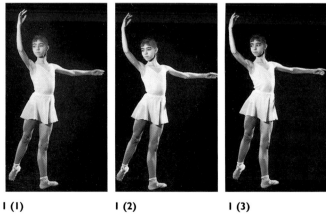

| I (1) | I (2) | I (3) |

Variants of the backward *effacé* are given in *photos 2a, 2b, 2c, 2d*.

The most common mistakes in executing this pose are as follows: insufficient strength in the support side causes the 2nd-position arm to go forward together with the shoulder *(photo 1(1))*, and the side of the working leg is clamped *photo 1(2))*.

**N. Ananiachvili and N. Liepa in "Coppélia".**

The body may be turned toward the working leg with a slight bend in the waist *(photos 1(2), 1(3))*.

The arm raised into the 3rd position may depart from the centre *(photo 1(3))*. The palm of the 3rd-position arm may be turned outside *(photo 1(1))*.

The *écarté* pose (from the French verb meaning "to move aside") is wide-opened and broad. It is recommended that its study should begin with the backward *écarté*. It has a bright and expressive design. The performer's entire figure is deployed in one diagonal direction (connecting in this case pts.8 and 4).

The leg stretched to toe or raised 90 degrees in the *écarté* is opened into a point which is distant from the spectator, producing the impression of moving away from him. The backward *écarté* is reached by the leg standing in front in position V.

One arm is raised to the 3rd position with the corresponding leg extended to toe *(Table 24, photo 1)* or raised to 90 degrees *(photo 2)*; the arm corresponding to the support leg is opened into the 2nd position, with the head turned towards it and eyes looking openly at the right hand. The 3rd-position arm, the body and the support leg form the core of the pose. A hollow back under shoulder blades and a body bend away from the raised leg are added later, in the third year.

Variants of the backward *écarté* pose are given in *Table 24, photos 2a, 2b, 2c*.

Various mistakes can be made in learning this complex pose: it is often performed as a simple *à la second* with no detail, no manifest turn or inclined head or hollow back under the shoulder blades or, on the contrary, with some exaggeration while impairing the precision of the *épaulement* and over emphasizing the head bend and the arching.

The 3rd position arm deviates from the centre *(photo 1 (2))*, its elbow is set out

**TABLE 24**

1

2

2 A

2 B

2 C

I (1)

I (2)

I (3)

insufficiently well, the shoulder is not fully lowered; the 2nd-position arm is advanced together with the shoulder *(photo 1(2)),* and the hand is "broken" at wrist *(photo 1(1), 1(2), 1(3)).* The graphic precision of the pose is impaired. The 2nd position arm's elbow is not kept up well enough. The head and body often lean towards the 3rd position arm *(photo 1(3))* or, on the contrary, have an excessive downward lean. In mastering the pose it is necessary to work for uprightness and gracefulness with a pulled-up trunk, precision of arm lines in positions, and balance in the pose's artistic outlook.

1. V. Morits, N. Tarasov, A. Chekrygin. *Metodika Klassicheskogo Trenazha* (Classical Dance Training Techniques), p.53.

*Arabesque,* one of the most expressive poses in classical dance (meaning, in French, an "ornament made of geometrical figures") is a combination of austere straight lines.

The pose's elongated shape is formed by the lines of a back-stretched leg and an arm opened forward into the *allongé* position. The head setup enhances the general sense of direction. "The head is not inclined together with the trunk, but is not leaned backwards either; the neck should not be outstretched while trying to give the head a certain impetus forward ...."[1]

**TABLE 25**

I      2

2 A      2 B      2 C

I (1)      I (2)      I (3)

**TABLE 26**

1

2

There are four forms of *arabesques* in the Soviet school of classical dance *(Table 26, photos 1, 2, 3 and 4)*.

The *arabesque 1* pose is marked by clarity, a forward thrust and an elongated outline. One arm is opened forward, the other sideways in the *allongé* position. The forward arm is positioned against the shoulder and at its level. The sideways arm is also against the shoulder and continues its line. The arms are smooth, slightly rounded at wrist and elbow, and opened to their entire length. The hands continue the arm line and seem to rest on air (the arm corresponding to the support leg is opened forward, while the sideways arm corresponds to the leg outstretched to toe or raised by 90 degrees). The eyes look far in front, past the finger tips. The support leg is half-turned outside *(Table 27, photos 1, 2)*.

The forward-opened arm gives direction to the entire pose. N. Tarasov recommended that in *arabesque 1* the forward arm should not be held fully horizontally, but so that the hand which continues the forward thrust of the arm should be at the eye level, while the sideways-opened arms should be "strictly horizontal" at the shoulder level. "The correct position of the arms plays a particularly important role in this pose," he wrote, "because if the forward arm is raised higher than the standard is, the arabesque's characteristic sense of direction if eliminated. It is also lost if the hand is up."[1]

Variants of the *Arabesque 1* Pose are given in *Table 27, photos 2a, 2b, 2c*.

The following mistakes are often made in learning the pose: the forward-opened arm intersects the central axial line and is clasped to the armpit *(photo 1(2))* or goes away from the shoulder *(photo 1(3))*. The sideways-opened arm may go back beyond the shoulder line *(photo 1(4))*. It could be either too low *(photo 1(3))* or too high

**TABLE 27**

1

**1.** V. Morits, N. Tarasov, A. Chekrygin. ***Metodika Klassicheskogo Trenazha*** (Classical Dance Training Techniques), p.53.

**3**

**4**

*(photo 1(4)),* with the hands strained and "broken" at the wrist.

In order to make it more convenient to control the evenness of shoulders and hips during the execution of *arabesques,* it is recommended that initially the pose should be trained in side view along a straight line. Only then should one go over to the learning of *arabesque 1* from the *épaulement* position. It is also recommended that students learning this pose should be turned full face to the mirror from time to time, in order to help them develop self-control.

In senior classes it is admissible for the sideways-opened arm to be a little behind the shoulder line, which gives the pose an added span *(Table 26, photos 1, 2, 3, 4).*

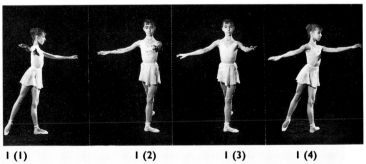

**2**

**I (I)**        **I (2)**        **I (3)**        **I (4)**

**A**        **2 B**        **2 C**

The design of *arabesque 2* is complicated and self-styled, marked by special gracefulness.

What gives direction to the pose is the forward-opened arm which corresponds to the leg stretched to toe *(Table 28, photo 1)* or raised 90 degrees *(photo 2)*. The line between the fingers of the forward-outstretched hand to the toes of the backward-outstretched foot gives the pose a sense of duration in time.

The arm opened sideways must be slightly visible from behind the shoulder as a result of a hollow under the shoulder blades *(photo 1, 2)*. The support leg is in the half-outside position. The head turned away from the general direction of the pose (with a soft neck outline) gives it a special nuance.

Variants of the *Arabesque 2* Pose are given in *photos 2a, 2b.*

The mistakes that are made in executing *arabesque 2* are most often due to the

**TABLE 28**

1

2

I (I)        I (2)        I (3)

2 A        2 B

*Bebezitche, the winner of the Moscow international competition, in the ballet "La Sylphide".*

incorrect position of the trunk. An insufficient back bend under the shoulder blades prevents the sideways-opened arm from reaching its place; the forward-opened arm is not held directly against the shoulder, but either crosses the vertical line that divides the trunk in two *(photo 1(2))* or is held aside from it *(photo 1(3))*. The forward-opened arm may be either clamped in the armpit *(photo 1(2))* or outstretched excessively far forward together with the shoulder *(photo 1(1))*. When the side of the working leg is clamped *(photo 1(3))* and the elbows are bent too much *(photo 1(2))*, there is a shade of affectation and mannerism in the pose.

Precision of outline in *arabesque 2* requires work on the correct trunk setup, a definite line going from the fingers of the forward-outstretched hand to the toes of the backward-outstretched foot, and a well-turned upper part of the trunk. It is recommended that *arabesque 2* should also be studied initially in side view along a straight line.

The outline and nature of *arabesque 3* are quite clear-cut, definitive and affirmative. The pose is formed from the *épaulement croisé* and, just like in the *croisé*, there is an emphasis on the crossing lines of the support leg and the working leg: one line stretches from the fingers of the forward-opened arm to the toes of the leg stretched to toe *(Table 29, photo 1)* or raised 90 degrees *(photo 2)*; the other line goes from the fingers of the sideways-opened arm to the shoulder of the forward-opened arm. A variant of this pose is given in *Table 29, photos 2a, 2b.*

What makes *arabesque 3* different from *arabesques 1* and *2* is that it requires the absolute outside of the support leg. The arms are directly against the shoulders, outstretched to their entire length, with the fingers reaching forward and the eyes looking beyond the fingers of the forward-opened arm. The forward-opened arm corresponds to the leg stretched to toe or raised 90 degrees, and the sideways-opened arm corresponds to the support leg.

Subsidence on the support hip is a common mistake in learning the *arabesque 3* pose *(photo 1(2))*. The working leg's side is often clamped. These errors cause uneven shoulders and the wrong level of arms. The sideways-opened arm is either higher *(photo 1(3))* or lower *(photo 1(1), 1(2))* than appropriate. The arms are too

**TABLE 29**

I  2

2 A  2 B

I (I)  I (2)  I (3)

bent at the elbows *(photo 1(1), 1(2)),* and the hands are drooping *(photo 1(1)).* The forward-opened arm is clamped at the armpit or, on the contrary, is held aside from the shoulder line. All of which impairs the graphic purity of the pose.

In mastering *arabesque 3* one should seek a high-standing support hip, shoulder blades pulled right down, and a shoulder well lowered toward the sideways-opened arm because this tends to be lifted.

*Arabesque 4* is one of the most dynamic, expressive and complicated poses in terms of its execution techniques, outline and artistic image.

The pose's expressiveness stems from a complex combination of the lines of the legs, arms, trunk, shoulders and a turned head. The pose is based on a strong twist of the upper trunk round the vertical axis towards the working leg with the hips in a fixed position. As a result of this twist, the forward-opened right arm in the *allongé* position, the shoulders and the sideways-opened left arm in the *allongé* position form an uninterrupted line connecting pts.8 and 4. The upper trunk tends to reach a crossing position with regard to the hip line. The hips are held along the diagonal line connecting pts.2 and 6, while the shoulders and arms are tending to form a line intersecting that diagonal (and connecting points 8 and 2). The trunk is held high, the back is slightly hollow under the shoulder blades, the head is turned toward the mirror, eyes looking in the same direction. It is a "winged" and flexible pose with a wide spread of the arms *(Table 30, photos 1, 2)*. Photo 2a shows a variant of *arabesque 4*.

Mistakes in executing *arabesque 4* are mostly associated with the complicated work of the trunk. Instead of turning the upper trunk from the waist up, students often place the forward-opened arm beyond the shoulder line *(photo 1(2))*, which breaks the straight line of the back, shoulders and arms.

The upper part of the trunk is not held upright, but is leaned forward as if in a fall, causing the forward-opened arm to be lowered *(photo 1(1))*. The trunk is not twisted separately from the hips, but together with them, and that makes the pose a flattened one and devoid of line interplay *(photo 1(3))*.

Another common mistake in this as in all other arabesques is the tensed and strained neck. A smooth and flexible line of the neck with the head set up appropriately should be the goal of training.

To master the trunk twist from the waist up, a very complicated motion, one should practise it in the full face position with the arms in positions 2 and 3 before actually starting work on the *arabesque 4* pose. In doing so, the object of training is the profile position of the upper trunk with regard to the full face position of the hips.

Unlike the above listed poses, the *attitude* is executed only by 90 degrees. The bent knee of the raised leg is the distinctive feature of this pose and one

**TABLE 30**

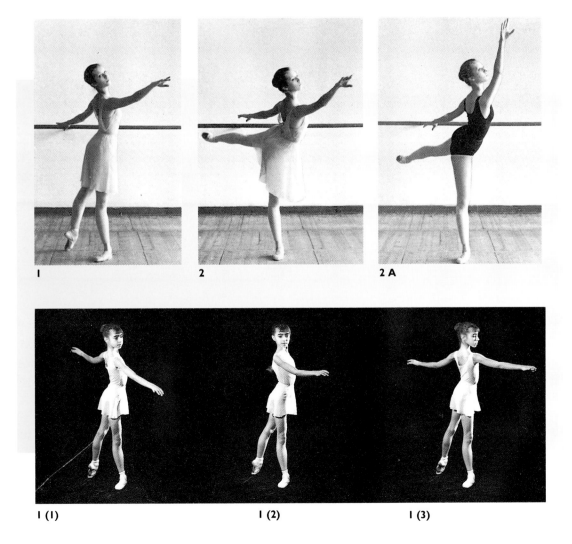

I      2      2 A

I (1)      I (2)      I (3)

**TABLE 31**

I  2

I A  I B  I C

2 A  2 B  2 C

that determines its imagery and visual structure. It is the bended knee that holds the trunk in this pose with a lesser bend forward than in the *arabesques,* and the outline of the back in the *attitude* is straighter and higher as a result. Unlike the *arabesque,* the attitude has a greater vertical than horizontal thrust.

The *attitude croisé* pose is very similar to the 90 degree backward *croisé (Table 31, photo 1).* It is a stable and affirmative pose. It differs from the *attitude effacé* also in that the leg bend angle is steeper and that the raised leg's line is less smooth. In the *attitude croisé* the knee is bent at a right

*Mario Liepa in "Chopiniana".*

angle, while the *attitude effacé* angle is obtuse.

The *attitude effacé* is analogous to the 90 degree backward *effacé (photo 2)* and has a flying nature.

Variants of the *attitude* pose are given in *Table 31, photos 1a, 2a, 2b, 1b, 1c, 2c.*

Mistakes made in learning the attitude are similar to those found in the *croisé* and 90 degree backward *effacé* poses. Apart from it, the hip of the raised leg may not be held firmly enough.

N. I. Tarasov believes that the distinction between major and minor poses is determined by the height to which the leg is raised. According to Tarasov, all the poses with a leg raised to 90 degrees are major poses. All those with the toes on the floor or a leg raised 45 degrees are minor poses.

Other authors (e.g. V. P. Mei, N. P. Bazarova, V. S. Kostrovitskaya) make the definitions of major and minor poses dependent on the height of the arms. By their definition, all the poses with arms in the third position are major poses. This principle is taught at the Moscow Ballet School.

It is clear that no pose with a leg raised to 90 degrees can be a minor one. But a pose with a leg stretched to toe can also be a major one. Variants of minor poses are given in *Table 32, photos 1, 2, 3.* Variants of major poses with toes on the floor are given in *photos 4, 5, 6, 7, 8, 9.*

**TABLE 32**

*N. Pavlova in "Giselle".*

*Arabesque from the ballet "Don Quixote".*

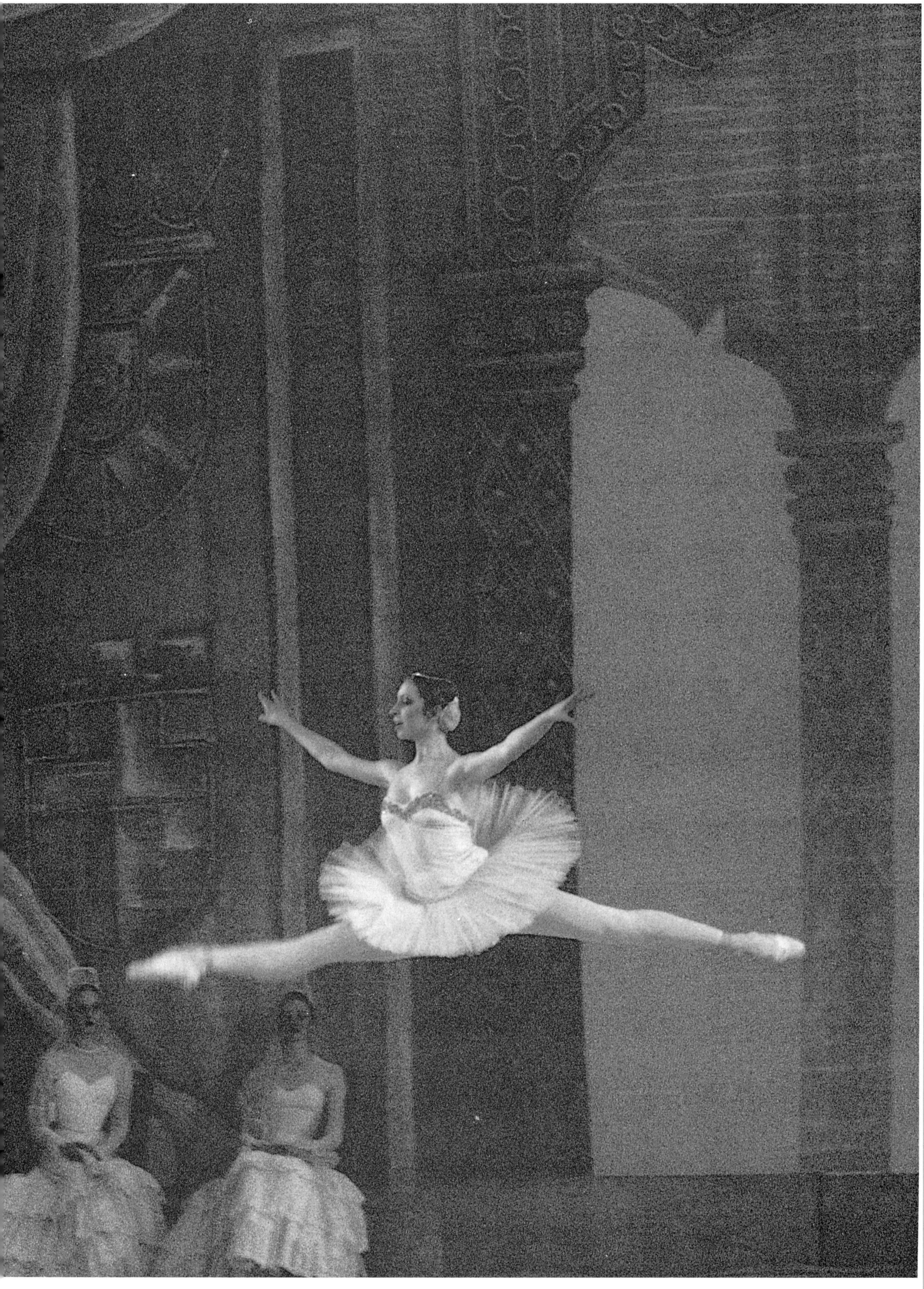

*The second
arabesque from
"The Nutcracker" –
free interpretation
by Nadejda Pavlova
and Vatcheslav
Gordeev.*

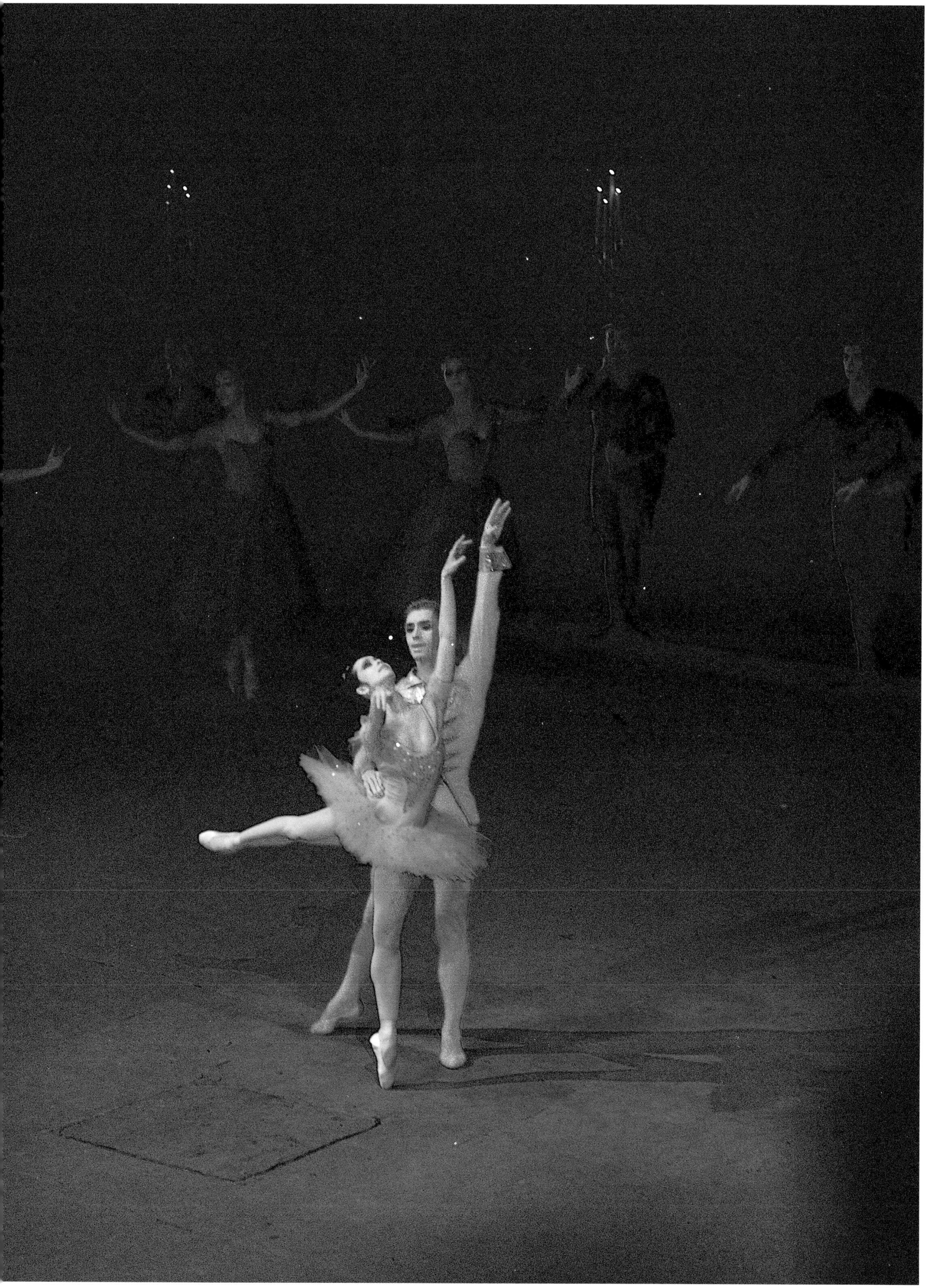

# MOVEMENT OF THE ARMS

Second act of "Swan Lake", performed by the Bolshoi company.

Pupils from the Bolshoi Academy of Dance.

*V. Derevianko in "Ces sons magiques" ["Those magical sounds"], music by Rameau. Choreography by V. Vassilyev.*

*The ballet "Paquita" performed by the Bolshoi Academy of Dance.*

# Basic Forms of
# *Port de Bras*

The study of arm positions – the basic elements of the *port de bras* and of poses– provides the ground for the student to learn the basic forms and different variants of the *port de bras.*

These forms affirm the independent significance and beauty of the movements of the arms, the trunk and the head. The practice is aimed at not only the correct transfer of the arms from one position to another, but also the beauty, imagery, artistic value, significance and dignity of each gesture. It is also an exercise allowing one to master in slow tempo the coordinative and artistic foundations of the highly complex virtuoso movements from the *adagio, allegro* and toe dance categories.

The *port de bras* has gone through significant changes in the development of classical dance techniques. What separates the Russian classical dance school from the Western European school is that is has developed the *port de bras* forms in a very broad and self-styled way. The basic *port de bras* forms have turned into a separate and serious stage of work on the arms. These forms are characterized by the wide amplitude of arm movements (associated with the twisted or bent trunk) and a high degree of coordination between the

movements of the arms and those of the trunk and head.

The basic forms and numerous variations of the *port de bras* developed by our most outstanding teaching masters is a means to broaden the expressive potential of the arm dance and to enhance and widen the arm motion's role in the general structural form of classical dance.

Described in this manual are the six basic forms of the *port de bras* that have been finalized in recent years in teaching theory and practice (although there are known to be other numberings and description terms of the basic *port de bras* forms). This manual also cites some variations of the *port de bras* developed by Ye. P. Gerdt and S. N. Golovkina, well-known teachers of the Moscow school.

The six *port de bras* forms are based on the variational development of motions from the simplest to the most complex.

The six *port de bras* forms have similarities and differences among them. What they have in common is their musical and visual structure, internal wave-like rhythm and unbroken manner of execution. They are different at the same time because each form has its own isolated completeness and integrity, in terms of musical and visual nuances.

Each form of the *port de bras* consist of two phrases. It starts from the same initial position, the *épaulement croisé*, and moves towards the apex of its development – a culmination which is expressed either in a definite posture or a definite fragment of motion – following which the movement comes to a resolution and softly returns to the starting position.

The phrasing of motion is a very subtle point. It depends on the nature of the musical accompaniment and in a large measure on the teacher's individuality, resulting in the different ways of treating the execution rules of certain *port de bras* forms (like the fifth or sixth) that are found in classical dance teaching books.

This is why we consider it inappropriate to give rigid instructions about certain accentuations of movement, but are only suggesting one of many possible treatments. In line with the logic of well-known textbooks, we will try to explain some characteristics of certain elements of motion.

Teachers should pay attention to those fragments of motion (present in every form of the *port de bras*) that are most complicated for execution or are described differently in various sources. Each *port de bras* has the most dynamic and expressive part which is the most difficult one for execution as a rule. We find it necessary for the teacher to call the student's attention to the most difficult segments of movement which are also the most important artistically, and to be very specific about his or her instructions and assignments when the minutest details of an artistic or technical nature are discussed.

---

The rules of executing the isolated elements of the *port de bras* mastered separately in the study of positions, are the same in the execution of the principal forms.

To perform the principal forms of the *port de bras*, a sense of the movement's imaginative, formal and musical integrity is crucial. The student's artistic talent and personality start to develop here at the earliest stage of training.

The first *port de bras*: *Table 33, photos a, b, c, d, e, f, g.*

The first *port de bras*, just as all other principal forms, is performed from the *épaulement croisé* with feet in position V (the right foot in front).

The arms rise from the preparatory position into the 1st and then 3rd position, open into the 2nd position and are then lowered into the preparatory position.

At the early stage of movement the eyes are looking at the palms; when the 1st position is reached, the head bends slightly to the left shoulder, and then the eyes and the movement of the head accompany the right arm's movement into the 3rd position; during their opening into the 2nd position and their subsequent lowering into the preparatory position the head turns to follow the right arm's movement. The eyes thus follow the right arm's movement.

**TABLE 33**

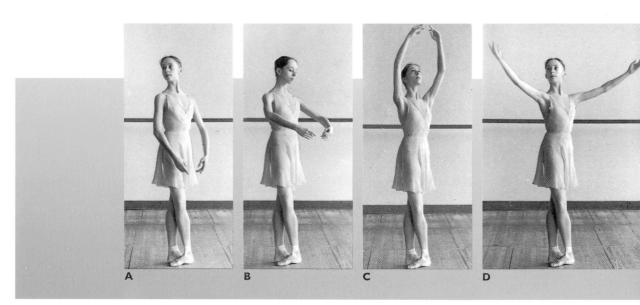

A          B          C          D

*N. Bessmertnova in the ballet "Giselle".*

F                    G

TABLE 34

A

B

C

D

E

A(1)

D

E

F

B(1)

C(1)

Second act from "Swan Lake".

*Performance given by pupils from the Bolshoi Academy of Dance.*

During the execution of this *port de bras* form the same rules should be observed for the lifting, lowering, opening and closing of arms as those which have been worked out in preparatory forms. The focus of attention when learning the *port de bras* form should be the coordination between the work of the arms and the *épaulement* position of the trunk.

To emphasize the culmination of movement – the highest point in its development – it is necessary to slow down the arm's motion before the 3rd position is achieved; the 3rd position should be delayed for a little while, as if hesitating before the next phase.

The second *port de bras*: *Table 34, photos a, b, c, d, e, f.*

The *préparation* is performed before the second *port de bras* (foot position V, the right foot in front); the left arm is opened from the preparatory position into the 3rd position, and the right arm into the 2nd position, both through the 1st position.

In the first year it is initially appropriate to work on the separate forms of the second *port de bras* (photos a, b, c, d, e, f). From the above described starting position the left arm is opened into the 2nd position (the left arm's movement begins as if from the glance of the eyes), and the head and the eyes accompany the left arm's motion to the 2nd position. Then the left arm is lowered into the preparatory position, with the right arm simultaneously lifted into the 3rd position, and the head is transferred to the right in a soft turn, with the eyes looking far beyond the right elbow. Then the arms are joined in the 1st position, the eyes are directed to the right palm and follow the right arm's movement, and the head is turned slightly to the left shoulder. Then the arms are opened into the initial position, the head turns toward the right hand, the eyes also watching the right hand.

The meaning and the beauty of this *port de bras* form consist in the circular motion of the arms striving towards a culmination point, when one arm is in the 3rd position and the other in the preparatory position (*photo c*).

What should be sought in this connection is the precise and beautiful work of the fingers and hand making a smooth, broad gesture, and the softly coordinated turn of the head repeating the circular movement of the arms.

In order to stress the culmination point of the movement completing its first phase the arms should somewhat slow down before attaining the main pose, so that after a moment's fixation there could be a quiet return to the initial position.

Later (in the 2nd year) the collective form of the second *port de bras* is studied (*photos d, e, a(1), b(1), c(1)*).

TABLE 35

From the above initial position both arms move in different directions: one *en dehors*, the other *en dedans* (*photos a(1) → b(1)*).

The difficulty of the transfer consist in the fact that both arms must move simultaneously at different speeds. For them to move simultaneously and to come to fixed points at the same time, the left arm must move twice as fast as the right arm, because its path is twice as long.

The third *port de bras* : *Table 35, photos a, b, c, d, e, f, g, h, i, j, k, l.*

The third *port de bras* is a more complicated version of the first one. Apart from the lifting and opening of the arms it includes a body bend forward and a bend back, which increases the amplitude of the movement.

The *préparation* is performed before the third *port de bras*; *épaulement croisé*, foot position V (the right foot in front, *photo a),* the arms open from the preparatory position through the 1st

position (*photo b)* into the 2nd position (*photo b),* the head is turned right, and the eyes are looking at the right hand. As the arms are lowered from the 2nd position into the preparatory position the body is bent forward from the waist, the head is turned right and the eyes are watching the right hand (*photos d, e, f).* Then, simultaneous with the lifting of the body, the arms are raised from the preparatory position through the 1st position into the 3rd position, with the head and eyes following the arm movement (*photos g, h).* After that the body is bent backward with the arms in the 3rd position (the head turned right – *photo i),* then, together with the lifting of the body, the arms are opened into the 2nd position in a broad and smooth gesture (the eyes watching the right arm – *photos j, k)* and are lowered into the initial preparatory position (*photo l).*

The 3rd position is the highest culmination point here as in the first *port de bras.* It is similarly stressed by the slow-down

E          F

K          L

preserve the 3rd position which is fixated. When the body has regained verticality, the arms are opened into the 2nd position in a separate movement.

Later, in the 2nd and 3rd years, the opening of the arms from the 3rd into the 2nd position and the return of the body into the vertical position after the back bend are performed simultaneously *(photos i, j, k)*. It is helpful to work on this form of the *port de bras* in the full face 1st position.

Some of the more well-known authors (like N. I. Tarasova, A. Ya. Vaganova, V. S. Kostrovitskaya, V. P. Mei and N. P. Basarova) believe that the angle of the body bend from the waist forward must correspond to that of the bend backward. But in today's teaching practice many such movements are executed more intensively: the bend forward in the *port de bras* must be completed with the maximum possible bow forward from the waist.

The fourth *port de bras*: *Table 36, photos a, b, c, d, e, f, g, h.*

The fourth *port de bras (photos a(1), b(1), c(1), d(1), e(1), f(1), g(1))* is more complex and dynamic than the previous forms and differs from them in the quality of the bend, which includes a turn of the trunk at the waist, so that the upper part of the body tends to reach a crossing position with regard to the hip line.

Initial position: *épaulement croisé*, foot position V (the right foot in front), the left arm in the 3rd position, the right arm in the 2nd position. The head is turned to the right, the eyes are looking at the right hand. From this position the left arm is opened into the 2nd position simultaneously with the body turn from the waist to the left, and the palm is turned gradually down. The turning head and the eyes accompany the movement of the left arm to pt.6, following which the body is turned further to the left, while the head is transferred to the right, and the eyes are meeting the movement of the right hand, which accompanies the body movement.

The turn of the upper part of the body is made against a fixed position of the hips. When the body and arm position is similar to the fourth *arabesque*, the arms and the shoulder blades must form one diagonal line from pt.8 to pt.4. The head is turned left to the mirror, the neck line is softened, there is a small hollow under the shoulder blades. Then, together with the return of the body into the initial position, the arms are joined in the 1st position (the eyes are looking at the right palm), following which they are

in the arm movement, a "sighing" pause in the 3rd position and the subsequent smooth bend and return to the initial position.

Some details require special attention in the study of this *port de bras*. When bowing forward, the arms must not lag behind the movement of the body, but always be a little in front of the shoulders *(Table 35, photo e)*. The head must not lag behind the body either, but bow together with it and complete the movement at the lowest point. Then it must go up simultaneously with the body. The shoulder blades' line must be smooth and not hump. During the rise the arms must move simultaneously with the body as if they are lifting it.

The return of the body back into the vertical stance following the bend back is the most difficult part of the movement. So, when learning the third *port de bras* in the first year, it is recommended that the lifting of the body and opening of the arms be done separately. During the rise the arms

TABLE 36

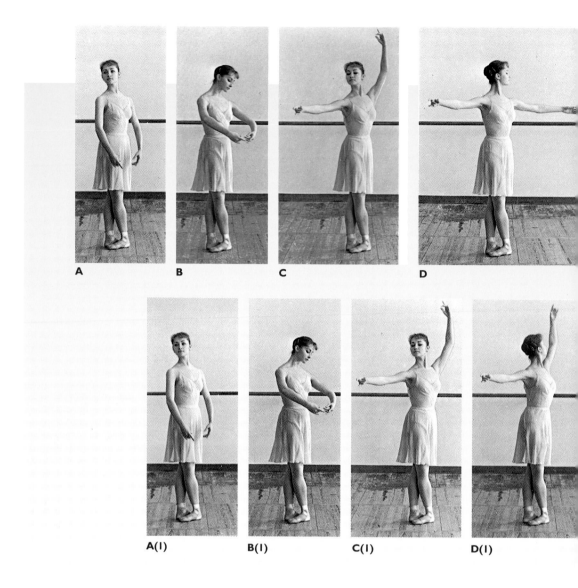

A  B  C  D

A(1)  B(1)  C(1)  D(1)

opened into the initial position, and the eyes are transferred to the right hand *(photo a(1), b(1), c(1), d(1), e(1), f(1), g(1))*.

The highest culmination point which the motion reaches in its development is the fourth *arabesque* position. The turn at the waist is the most dynamic and expressive fragment of the movement, and is executed in complex coordination with the movement of the head and the eyes.

The teacher should give maximum detail in explaining this fragment.

The opening of the left hand from the 3rd into the 2nd position is started as if from the movement of the head, which is lifted, with the eyes looking at the left hand *(photos c(1) → d(1))*. The smooth progress of the left hand is followed by a corresponding turn of the head and by the eyes up to pt.6 *(photo d(1))*. After that the head makes a soft, round movement to the right and the eyes are directed to meet the right arm's movement, while the upper body continues to turn left. In order to emphasize

the culmination of the fourth *port de bras*, there must be a little slow-down in the progress of the body and arms before the fourth *arabesque* position is attained. When performing this part of the motion, the right hand must lag behind the whole arm a little and "cut" the air in a slower movement, as if it were a fish fin. The culmination point must be emphasized with a soft hollow under the shoulder blades, making the final point in the pose, and a small pause in the fourth *arabesque* pose *(photo e(1))*.

Following that the movement returns to the initial position as if calming down.

Since the body turn from the waist with the simultaneous opening of the arms is the most complicated element of the fourth *port de bras*, there is a need to work on it in stages.

Before the aggregate form of the fourth *port de bras* is studied, it is useful to learn a less complex one. From the above described initial position the left arm is opened into the 2nd position, the eyes and head

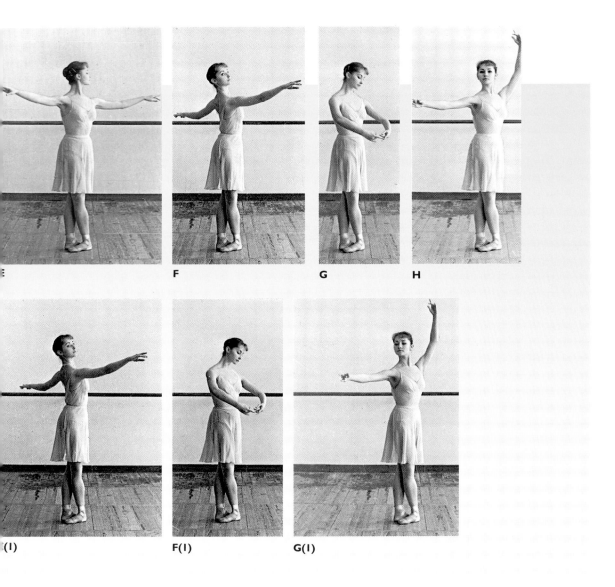

E    F    G    H

(I)    F(I)    G(I)

following its movement, but the body remains immobile. Then the trunk is turned from the waist to the left, during which the hands are turned palms down with a light "sigh" and, slightly behind the arms, follow them. The head turns to the right.

This form of the fourth *port de bras* differs from the complete one in that the body turn and the opening of the arms are done alternately, and not simultaneously in one combination *(photos c, d, e, f, g, h)*.

Mistakes in performing the fourth *port de bras*, just like the fourth *arabesque*, are most often made during the turn of the body from the waist, and result in the lack of simultaneity in the work of the body, arms and head. The right arm is put too far in front. The hips fail to remain in a fixed state and are turned to follow the upper part of the body.

It is useful to work separately on this complicated element.

The initial position is foot position I *en face*, the arms are opened into the 2nd

position. The body turns from the waist in profile with regard to the mirror, the hands turn palms down as they accompany the turn. When turning the body to the right, the head turns left and the eyes are looking beyond the left shoulder. Then the body is returned to the initial position, and the arms are placed in the 1st position.

A second version of the auxiliary exercise: initial foot position I *en face*, the arms in the 3rd position. During the body turn from the waist the arms are opened into the 2nd position, the hands turn palms down, then the body returns to the initial position, and the arms into the 1st position.

The fifth and sixth *port de bras* were described by Vaganova as "very important in our education. Having mastered them, a dancer can say to herself that she has found agreement between the head, the arms and the body, and has made a big step in mastering the body play."[1]

1. A. Ya. Vaganova. *Osnovy Klassicheskogo Tantsa* (Fundamentals of Classical Dance), p. 63.

The fifth and sixth *port de bras* develop flexibility, expression and require a very subtle artistic finishing of detail.

Unlike the previous forms, the fifth *port de bras* includes a circular body bend together with transfer of the arms from one position to another. This considerably increases the amplitude and volume of spatial design and strengthens the dynamics and expression of the movement.

The fifth *port de bras* is given in *Table 37, photos a, b, c, d, e, f, g, h, i, j, k, l, m, n.*

Before the fifth *port de bras* the following *préparation* is executed: foot position V (the right foot in front), the arms are opened through the 1st position, the left arm into the 3rd position, the right arm into the 3rd position, and the head is turned to the right.

From this position the arms expand the motion and are opened from the fingers, the head is transferred forward, the chin is lifted a little, the eyes look at the left palm (the opening of fingers begins from the eyes). Then the body is bent forward from the waist, at the same time the left arm is lowered into the 1st position (eyes watching it), while the right arm is brought to the left one and into the 1st position through the preparatory position. After the body regains verticality (the arms in the 1st position) it is turned left at the waist, and this turn progresses into a side bend. The eyes are watching the left arm, the head is also turned left. The side bend transforms into a back bend, and after the deepest point is reached (pt.4 in this example) the arms are transferred (right into the 2nd position, left into the 3rd position) as the body returns to the initial position. The head is turned to the right, and the eyes are shifted to the right arm, too.

The culmination in the development of the movement is the circular bend. This fragment can be considered as the acme of the fifth *port de bras*, its most expressive, dynamic and difficult part in terms of coordination. Unlike the previously-

**TABLE 37**

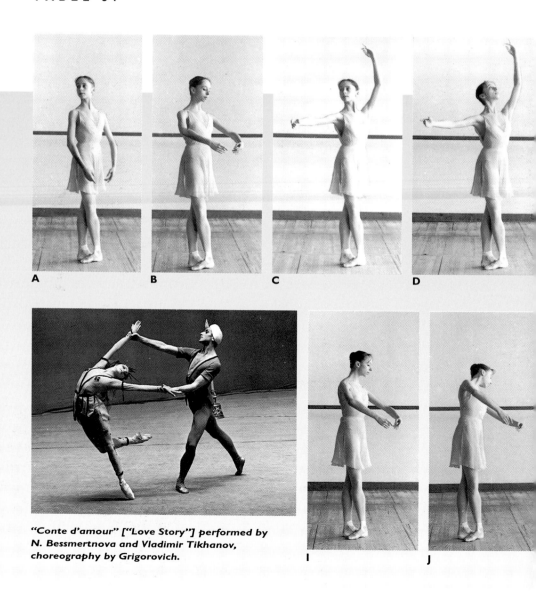

A    B    C    D

*"Conte d'amour" ["Love Story"] performed by N. Bessmertnova and Vladimir Tikhanov, choreography by Grigorovich.*

I    J

mastered forms, where the culmination is at the end of the first phrase, the culmination in the fifth *port de bras* is shifted toward the beginning of the second phrase and is not expressed by a pose, but by a fragment of the movement *(photos h, i, j, k, l, m)*.

Different interpretations of the rules of executing the fifth *port de bras* can be encountered and, consequently, different educational practices. This applies in the first place to the beginning of the circular bend. According to some teachers, including Ye. N. Geidenreich (who conducted seminars on teaching methods at the Moscow Ballet School), the fifth *port de bras* circular bend should be started from a small turn in the waist (by one-eight, *photos h , i),* followed by a back bend through the left side *(photos j, k)*. According to N. I. Tarasov, however, this element should be started from a "circular deviation aside". It appears that the different interpretations stem from divergences in male and female performance. What N. Tarasov suggests is a

more austere design. Other authors accentuate the bending turn which begins from a small turn at the waist. However, it should not be overdone. The turn must not be as active as in the fourth *port de bras*. It is necessary to begin the circular bend from a slight turn at the waist, which should then transform into a side bend and a subsequent bend back. Only then will this subtle artistic detail embellish the movement.

When working on the fifth *port de bras*, attention should be paid to some particularly difficult coordination aspects to prevent possible mistakes.

It often happens during the body bow that the head lags behind the trunk, the back "humps" at the waist or the shoulder blades, or that the arms in the 1st position are brought left separately from, and instead of, the body. During the back bend the arms are often transferred from one position into another either too early or too late, and the left hand returns to the initial position with some delay. It is necessary to watch that the

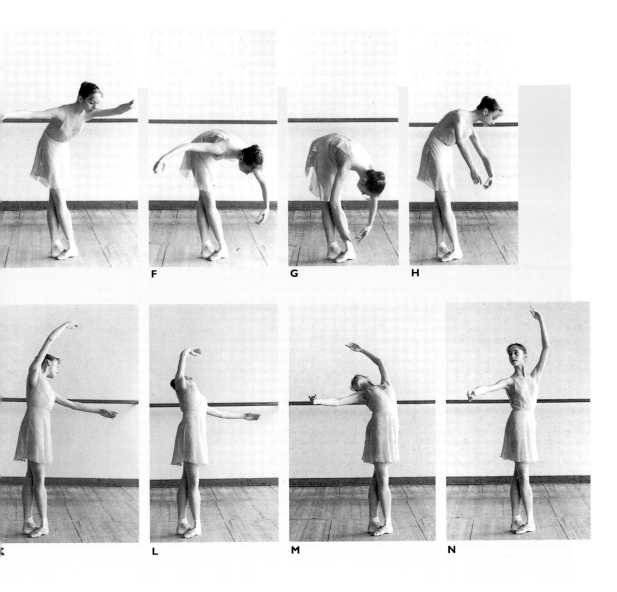

F          G          H

K          L          M          N

arms are changed only after the deepest bending point.

In order to avoid these mistakes, it is helpful to work out the first part of the movement separately from the second part at the initial stage. The student's attention should be called to the phase of movement where the change in the arm position takes place. It is necessary to see that the head is also lowered during the body bend forward and that it "finishes" the movement of the trunk and the lowest point.

The sixth *port de bras*

This is the most dramatic of the basic *port de bras* forms in terms of its spatial design, character and execution techniques. Its musical, rhythmical and visual structure includes dynamism, expression and power. It was not by chance that A. Vaganova used to call it the *grand port de bras*.

The sixth *port de bras*: Table 38, photos *a, b, c, d, e, f, g, h, i, j, k, l.*

The sixth *port de bras* can be viewed as a form of the fifth one with more complicated coordination. Apart from the elements of the fifth one, it includes a deep *demi-plié* (stretch-out) on the support leg and a transfer from one leg to the other, which considerably adds amplitude to the movement.

A *préparation* is executed before the beginning of the sixth *port de bras*. From the initial position (*épaulement croisé*, foot position V, the right foot in front) there is a transfer into the backward *croisé* with the toe of one foot on the floor, from one leg to the other through position IV on the "free" knees. Then the eyes are transferred to the left arm.

The *port de bras* starts from a deep *demi-plié* on the support leg and a simultaneous body bend forward, during which the arms preserve their initial position (the left one in the 3rd position, the right in the 2nd position). Then the left hand is slowly lowered into the 1st position, while the working foot slides on the floor with outstretched toes. The head and the eyes follow the left arm's movement *(photos d, e)*. After a maximum body bend *(photo e, f)* a push by the support leg shifts the centre of gravity to the left leg, the right leg following the transfer remains stretched forward to toe, the arms are joined in the 1st position, and the eyes are looking at the right palm. A circular bend follows (similar to the fifth *port de bras, photos h, i, j, k),* followed by a transfer to the right leg into the initial position, with the eyes and head turned to the right arm.

TABLE 38

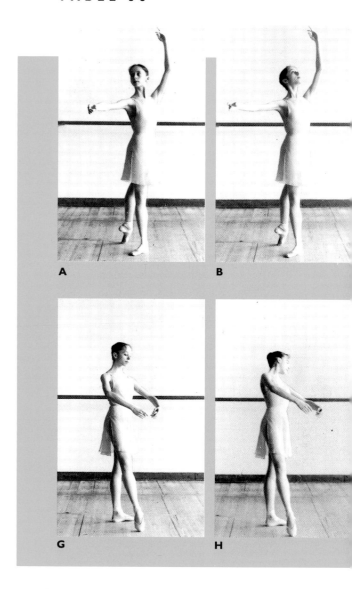

The culmination in this *port de bras* seems to grow out and include the end of the first phrase and the beginning of the second – the transfer from one leg to the other with the subsequent bend to the lowest point *(photos e, f, g, h, i, j, k, l).*

There are differences in the ways in which different authors describe the rules for the execution of the sixth *port de bras* and the necessary accentuations. A. Ya. Vaganova, for example, gives a more thoroughly artistic version of performance. In describing the rules for the shift from one leg to the other, she describes the dynamics and even expression of this complicated power element. "Having reached position IV, widened with as strong an effort as your constitution allows, straighten up the trunk and simultaneously throw it over to the left foot toes, with the head drawn back over the left shoulder,"[1] she wrote.

1. A. Ya. Vaganova. *Osnovy Klassicheskogo Tantsa* (Fundamentals of Classical Dance), p.62.

Different authors give different descriptions of the arms' travel during the leg transfer. A. Vaganova and V. Kostrovitskaya recommend that the arms should be put into the 1st position at the deepest stretch-out point right before the leg transfer. N. Tarasov, V. Mei and V. Bazarova believe that the arms should be put into the 1st position at the transfer point. Both approaches have logic behind them. If you follow the logic of the fifth *port de bras,* the arms in the sixth *port de bras* should be brought together at the lowest stretching point. But if you consider that the transfer from one leg to the other is a difficult power element in which the arms should actively assist, then it is more justifiable to put them together during the transfer. Both versions are legitimate. It should be noted, however, that in the former case the arms are brought together into the 1st position directly before the transfer from one leg to the other.

In the latter case it is necessary to watch that the body and arm movement is not stopped at one point, and the stretch-out must be completed with the lowering of the head, so that there is no "sticking" in one position at the lowest point of the stretch-out.

The student's attention should also be called to a few more coordinative elements of this *port de bras.*

During the ultimate body bend and the deep *demi-plié* on the support leg it should be ensured that the body, the head and the back-stretched leg should form one sloping line going up from the toes to the head *(photos d, g).* The clarity of this line is often impaired by the insufficient strength of the back and the hips: the hips and the sacrum are often raised higher than is admissible, the upper back stoops and the head is not held at the same level with the trunk (it is either lower than the back line, or too high), while the centre of gravity is shifted backwards beyond the support leg.

The second complicated element is the circular bend with the foot opened to toe, during which it is difficult to keep the hips even and immobile (they are most often shifted at the initial stage of learning, causing the forward-opened leg to lose its turnout and direction). To avoid mistakes in these complicated elements, it is recommended that before the sixth *port de bras* is studied, the third *port de bras* should be worked out thoroughly with stretch-out as a preparation for the fifth form, as well as the circular bend with a forward-opened leg.

The above *port de bras* forms should be studied as such in the first three years of training: the first, second and third form in the first year, the fourth and fifth in the second year, the third *port de bras* with stretch-out and the sixth *port de bras* in the third year.

*"Clair de Lune", music by Claude Debussy, choreography by L. Jdanov, T. Matatch and D. Sikorska.*

*The ballet "Meditation" with music by Massenet, choreography by K. Goleizovski, with A. Mikhalchenko and F. Anissimov.*

# Variations of
# *Port de Bras*

New tasks normally emerge at every stage of training. In the junior classes the study of the *port de bras* involves the elementary rules of raising, lowering, opening or closing the arms; in intermediate and senior classes the functions of these movements will change. Apart from continued work on the fundamentals of bodily setup, the *port de bras* training in intermediate classes seeks to develop a "singing" upper body, bodily cantillation, which is particularly important in *adagio*; on the other hand, there is an emphasis on agility and coordination which are so necessary in the *allegro* and toe dance. All the *port de bras* serve to streamline the travel of the arms, the transfers, bends and turns of the trunk which will later combine with quick and sharp leg movements in jumps, toe dance and rotations with a faster tempo and different accentuations. Unless all these numerous transfers are worked out meticulously in a slow manner beforehand, the arms are going to move in a chaotic and slovenly way, especially at passing moments, as they are going to be involved in complicated virtuoso movements.

The old masters of dance teaching did know the secrets of developing beautiful arms and expressive torsos in their students and of making them work in perfect coordination with leg movements. The archives of the MAKhU museum, which give an idea of Ye. P. Gerdt's work on the *port de bras*, make it possible for her experience to be used in today's education.

Beginning from the junior classes, Ye. Gerdt did not only teach the academic *port de bras*, where the arms move strictly through positions, but also various non-traditional versions. The body and head were actively involved in those *port de bras*, and they enabled the students to reveal their natural artistry, coordination and expressiveness.

Simultaneously with that, certain other details were studied and presented in a manner which made them interesting and understandable for children of that age (those details included the almost indetectable movements of fingers, hands and wrists during the raising and lowering of arms).

The following are two variations of the *port de bras* which Ye. Gerdt included in her junior class lessons.[1]

One variation, called "Scales" by Ye. Gerdt, served to develop a sense of

1. S. S. Kholfina. *Port de Bras v Klasse Ye.P. Gerdt* (Port de Bras in Ye. P. Gerdt's Classes). – *Bulleten Metodkabineta MAKhU* (Bulletin of MAKhU Teaching Methods Division). No. 2, Moscow, 1958/59, p.58.

linkage and smoothness in the transition of movement from one arm to the other. The concept of *legato* was introduced together with it. The main theme of the movement is rocking *(Table 39, photos a, b, c, d, e, f)*.

*Préparation*: arms are opened from the preparatory position *(photo a)* through the 1st position *(photo b)* into the 2nd position *(photo c)*, then hands turn into the *allongé* position *(photo d)*.

The right arm is lowered into a downward 2nd position with a sigh of the hand, the body bends slightly to follow the arm (slightly forward from the waist) to the right, and the head and the eyes also follow the arm's movement; the wrist is slightly softened. Simultaneously with that, the left arm is lifted into the upward 2nd position, with the hand slightly behind *(photo e)*.

accompanying the arm, also begin to turn left into pt.8; the chin is a little lowered, the eyes are watching the left hand *(photo b)*. Then the left arm is opened from the elbow forward into pt.8, the hand is opened with palm up (the left arm's gesture reminiscent of a salutation), and the head and eyes follow the arm's movement *(photo c)*.

Simultaneously the right arm, in an accompaniment to the left arm's movement, is opened palm up into the 2nd position. Following that both arms are drawn into the 2nd position, the palms are turned to a state corresponding to the 2nd position, and the body is straightened *en face*. Then both palms are turned down *(photo d)* and the entire exercise is repeated in the right-hand direction *(photos d, e, f)*.

**TABLE 39**

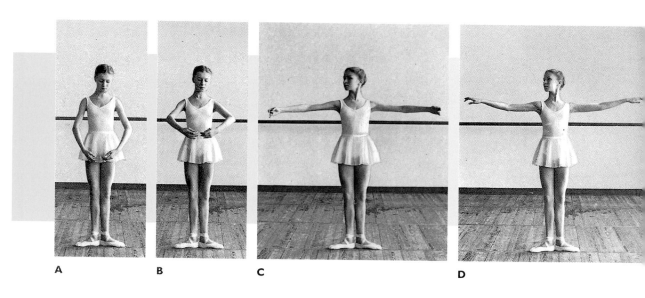

A          B          C                    D

After the culmination is achieved, marked by a short pause, the left arm, with a sigh of the hand, goes into the lower 2nd position, and the head and the body are slightly bent to the left to follow the left arm's movement (photo f). The right arm simultaneously goes into the upward 2nd position. The movement can be repeated several times.

Another example of the *port de bras* can serve to prepare the arms for certain kinds of toe dance and jumping movements with rather complicated coordination (Table 40, photos a, b, c, d, e, f).

*Préparation*: foot position I *en face*. The arms are raised from the preparatory position into the 2nd position palms down (photo a). The left arm begins to bend into the 1st position (part of the arm from the fingers to the elbow is lowered palm down). The body and the head, in a movement

**TABLE 40**

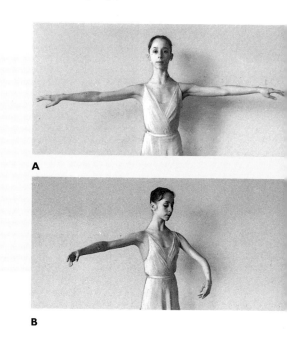

A

B

When this *port de bras* is executed, the movement passes continuously from one arm to the other, whereas the movement of each arm is a kind of accompaniment to the other. The resulting effect is cantillation. This *port de bras* trains gesture and helps younger pupils to absorb, in a digestible form, the concepts of legato, cantillation and the complex coordination between the body and arm dance.

The extent to which work on arms should be intensive, sophisticated and artistry-oriented in the middle and senior classes, can be judged from those version of the *port de bras* that Ye. P. Gerdt practised with her students. These examples give an idea of how necessary it is that the teacher should display his or her own artistry, pedagogical skills and ability to make oneself understood. One can see how purposefully the teacher prepares the students' bodies for the whole set of techniques which form the secrets of the trade, the entire palette of colours and shades in which classical dance is so rich.

Following the concept of legato, taught to junior students on the example of a small dance phrase, the teacher goes further to work out the cantillation principle in the middle classes. Examples of medium-level *port de bras* are combinations of movements, but each constitutes a rather long segment of music and dance.

The MAKhU archives give one the idea of how logical the transfers are in those *port de bras*, how beautiful their intricate pattern is, being made up of soft and smooth transfers of the body and arms. They show what purpose the teacher is seeking and how insistently she works on bringing up a sense of the inseparable link between the movement of the arms, body, feet and head, whose aggregate sum can give birth to "a flight full of soul", the famous "bel canto adagio" for which the Russian and Soviet classical ballet school is so famous. The traditions of arm training laid down by Ye. P. Gerdt are living and being developed further in the practical activity of the Moscow School today. Given here are Ye. P. Gerdt's variations of the *port de bras* which serve as preparations for more complex movements in terms of

F

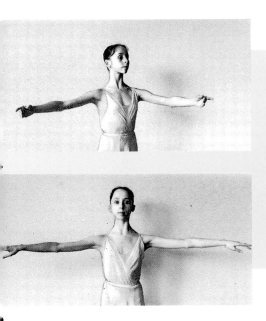
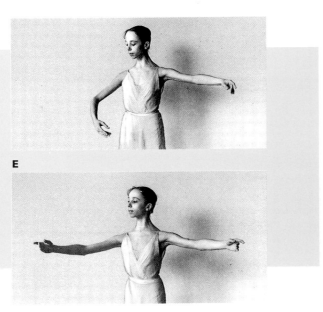

E

F

TABLE 41

A

B

C

D

E

F

G

H

I

J

K

L

**TABLE 42**

MOVEMENT OF THE ARMS **119**

coordination, and also different variants of the linking movements of the body and arm in the *adagio, allegro (Table 42, photos, a, b, c, d, e, f, g, h, i)* and toe dance *(Table 41, photos a, b, c, d, e, f, g, h, i, j, k, l)*.

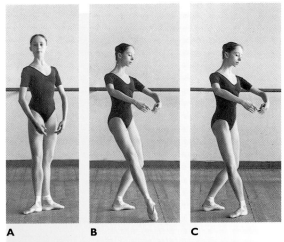

A          B          C

As in all movements of classical dance, there are great capabilities inherent in the *port de bras*. During the later phases of training, the movements can become more varied and complicated. There is more complex coordination, more difficult execution techniques and a greater variety of imaginative and artistic colouring. While being a separate section of study in the junior classes, the *port de bras* is normally

D          E          F          G

studied in the intermediate and senior classes as an element in combination with all other exercise sections, and therefore permeates them. The *port de bras* plays a specially important role in the *adagio*. It forms the imaginative and coordination basis of such movements as the *fouetté en effacé, renversé, grand fouetté et tournant*, which are carried over from the *adagio* section to the *allegro* and toe dance sections.

Given below are variations of the *port de bras* for middle and senior classes included in her lessons by S. N. Golovkina, a well-known modern teacher. These *port de bras* reveal a continued tendency embodied in the art of the outstanding Moscow school teachers Ye. P. Gerdt, M. A. Kozhukhova and N. I. Tarasov. Golovkina's *port de bras* can give an idea of how this movement can be made more complex in terms of execution and dramatics.

The first *port de bras* version is the simpler combination for middle classes *(Table 43, photos a, b, c, d, e, f, g, h)*, while the second one is a relatively more complex *port de bras* variation for middle classes.

H          I

***Example 1.***

Foot position V, right foot in front, *épaulement croisé (photo a)*. The second *port de bras* is executed *(photos a, b, c, d, e, f)*. After the arms are put together in the 1st position *(photo g)*, there is a turn into the backward *effacé* facing pt.2 *(photo h)*, during which the left leg is stretched back to toe on the floor in the *battement tendue* technique. The arms, which retained the 1st position

TABLE 43

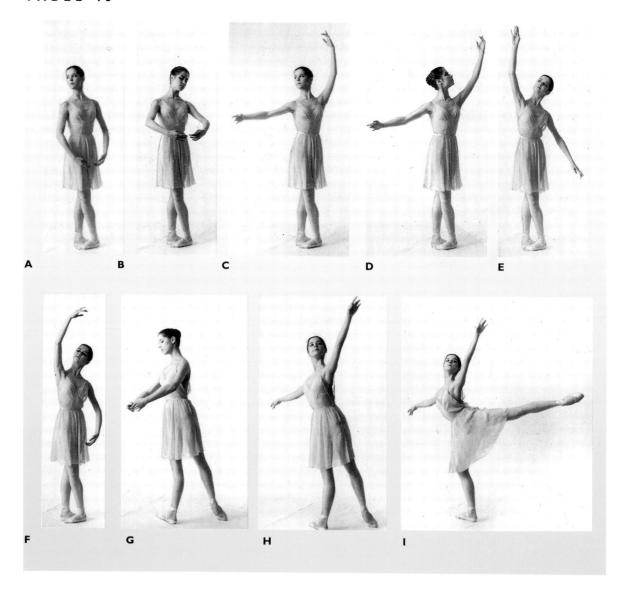

A B C D E

F G H I

during the turn *(photo g)*, are opened into the *allongé* pose, and the eyes look at the left hand *(photo h)*. The left foot is then closed into position V, and everything is repeated from the other foot.

Another version of this *port de bras* is made more complex because the left leg is raised 90 degrees in the *relevé lent* technique into the *allongé* pose, while the other arm is in the *demi-plié* (photo i).

**Example 2.**

The first version of the *port de bras* for intermediate classes: *Table 43, photo a, b, c, d, e, f.*

Foot position V (right foot in front) *en face. A soutenu* is executed sideways with the left foot set to toe on the floor, the body bending at the waist to the side of the working leg, with the arms simultaneously raised in the 2nd position (hands in the *allongé* position) and the shoulders taking a slanted position *(photo b)*. Then the body is stretched out of the *demi-plié* and

straightened, then it is bent over from the waist to the left into pt.3, during which the left arm is transferred from the 2nd into 3rd position *(photos c → d)*, the right arm from the 2nd into 1st position *(photo c → d)*, and the eyes watching the left arm's movement are shifted to the right. A *fouetté en dehors* follows with the toe on the floor by one-eighth into pt.8 and the forward *effacé* pose *(photos e → f)*, during which the right arm, slightly bent down from the elbow, moves toward the 1st position. Then both arms are transferred, opening from the elbows: the right arm forward, the left up (hands in the *allongé* ) , and the body is slightly bent back from the shoulder blades *(photo f)*. Following that, the left foot stands in position V forward, *épaulement croisé* at pt.2, and everything is repeated from the other foot.

A second version of this *port de bras* for middle classes can be used for senior classes

*The ballet "Paquita" by pupils from the Bolshoi Academy of Dance.*

## TABLE 44

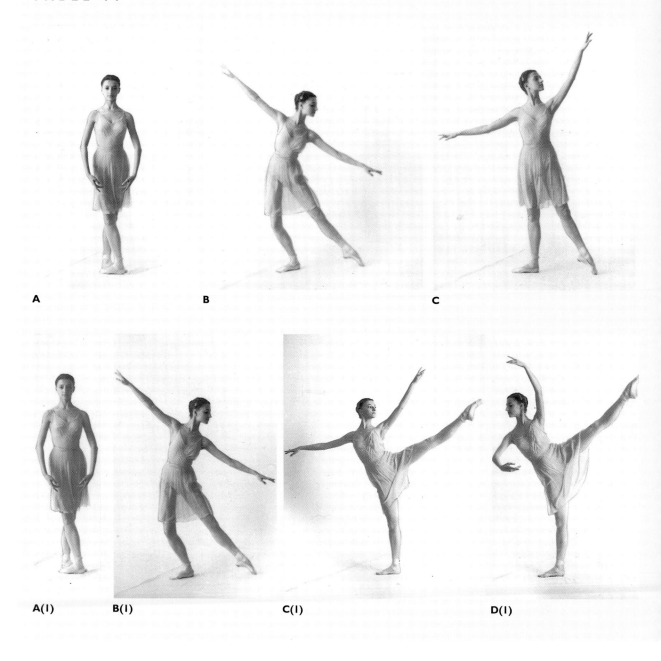

A    B    C

A(I)    B(I)    C(I)    D(I)

**Performance by pupils from the Bolshoi Academy of Dance. Choreography by M. Martirosyan.**

because the initial form becomes more complicated here *(photos a(1), b(1), c(1), d(1), e(1), f(1), g(1), h(1))*. After the left foot has opened in the *soutenu* technique with the toe on the floor, it is raised in a *relevé lent* to 90 degrees *à la second*, with arms in the *allongé* position *(photos b(1) → c(1))*. A bend follows towards the support leg, during which the left arm from the *allongé* is closed into the 3rd position, and the right arm into the 1st position *(photo d(1))*. Then the left leg is opened through the *passé* position by 90 degrees *(photo e(1))*, arms in the 1st position, eyes watching the left palm) into the forward *effacé* pose by 90 degrees into pt.8 *(photo f(1))*.

**D**     **E**     **F**

*Béjart's "Romeo and Juliet", performed by Y. Maximova and J. Don.*

**E(I)**     **F(I)**     **G(I)**     **H(I)**

The working leg can be transferred into any pose through a *passé*, e.g. into the third *arabesque (photos g(1) → b(1)).*

The transfer of arms in these *port de bras* looks more artistic than in junior classes. It is no longer necessary that the arms should go through the 1st position in transitional phases. As in the above example, they can go from the 3rd or 2nd position directly into the next position, only tending to reach the 1st position by being rounded from the elbows down a little more *(photos d, e, f).*

The second version of the *port de bras* is an example showing the ever-more complex logic of the *port de bras* in its development. We can see how the original version of the movement can be transposed into a more complex form employed in senior classes. The more complex versions appear to enhance the pitch of the *port de bras* by being executed in combination with a leg raised 90 degrees. These *port de bras* contain the idea of development which constitutes the basis of training.

*Bessmertnova and Lavrovski in a performance of "Giselle".*

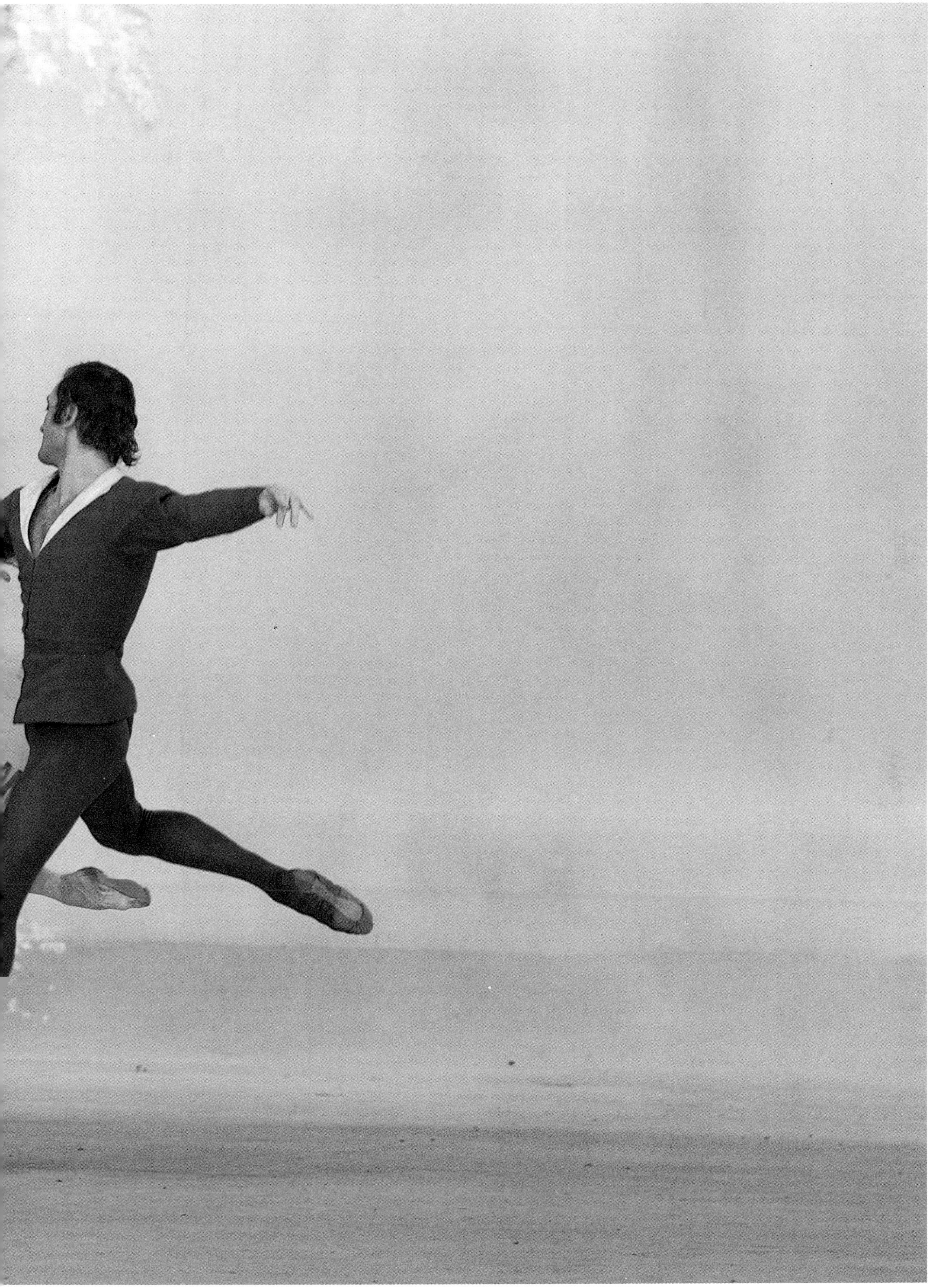

*N. Bessmertnova (Chirine) in the ballet "La Légende d'amour".*

*Right:*
*N. Bessmertnova and A. Bogatyrev in "La Légende d'amour". Choreography by Y. Grigorovitch.*

# Appendix

GUERDT, Elizavéta Pavlovna (17 April 1881 - 6 November 1975. Ballerina, teacher.

Daughter of Pavel Guerdt, lead dancer at the Marie Theatre (Mariinski), and the dancer Chapochnikova.

From 1908 to 1927, dancer at the Mariinski Theatre at St Petersburg, later to become the Kirov Theatre of Leningrad.

The noble and rigorous style of her dance was inspired by the best classical traditions of Ch. Johansson, M. Petipa and P. Guerdt. In Petipa's ballets, she performed the parts of Odette-Odile *(Swan Lake)*, Aurora *(The Sleeping Beauty)*, the princess *(The Little Hump-backed Horse)*, Nikia *(La Bayadère)*, and Paquita *(Paquita)*. In Fokine's ballets, she performed Armida *(Le Pavillon d'Armide)*, Sylphide *(Les Sylphides)*, and Columbine *(The Carnival)*.

After her career as a dancer, E. Guerdt devoted her time to various teaching activities. From 1927 to 1934, she taught at Leningrad School of Dance and also at the Kirov Theatre. From 1935 to 1975, while teaching at the Moscow School of Dance, she led an advanced proficiency class at the Bolshoi. She sought to pass on to her pupils her extensive stage experience and to instil in them high professional standards and good artistic taste. A. Chelest, M. Plisetskaya, R. Stroutchjova, V. Bovt and Y. Maximova are among her pupils. Her teaching methods involved many practical exercises.

Maria Taglioni made her début in 1822. She first played la Sylphide in 1832.

Carlotta Grisi performed Giselle in 1841.

Pierina Legnani performed Odette-Odile for the first time in 1895.

Anna Pavlova (1881-1931). In 1909 she performed in *Swan Lake.* Marina Semionova performed in *Swan Lake* between 1925 and 1930.

Maya Plisetskaya made her debut in 1943. She performed in *Swan Lake* in the 1950s.

YUSSIM Margarita Naoumovna. Born on 17 April 1937, she was a dancer, teacher and theatre historian.

After attending N. Dovguelian's class at the Tashkent Dance School (1954), she became a solo performer at the Tashkent Theatre of Opera and Ballet. She performed the role of Myrta in *Giselle,* the Lilac Fairy in *The Sleeping Beauty,* Zarema in *The Fountain of Bakhschisaray*, and Fleur-de-Lis in *Esmeralda.*

In 1966, she finished her studies in the history of the theatre at the State Institute of Art and Theatre (GITIS), where she studied under the direction of P. Markov. Her final-year thesis was devoted to the works of Kassian Goleizovski and was published in 1984 in a collection of articles on this maestro of ballet.

She was the author of a series of articles on the history of dance theory, published in magazines such as *Théâtre, Sovietski Balet,* and others.

From 1968 to 1990, she taught classical dance and was in charge of dance theory classes at the Moscow School of Dance. She helped draw up the teaching programmes for classical dance in 1977 and 1987.

Among her pupils were M. Ivanova, V. Tsoi, O. Kotovskaia, N. Malandina, and O. Tavetnitskaia.

GOLOVKINA, Sofia Nikolaievna, born 30 October 1915. Ballerina, teacher, choreographer. She studied at the Moscow School of Dance under A. Tchkryguine before becoming a dancer with the Bolshoi from 1933 to 1959, and performed, amongst other roles, that of the princess, Raymonda, Svanilda, Kitri, Zarema, and Odette-Odile. From 1959, she was director of Moscow Academic Dance School. Among her pupils were N. Bessmertnova, N. Sorokina, M. Leonova, A. Mikhaltchenko, O. Souvorova, G. Stepanenko, and N. Gratcheva. Author of a manual entitled *Lessons in Classical Dance* (1989).

ZOLOTOVA, Natalia Victorovna, born 7 May 1928. Ballerina and teacher. In 1945, she finished her studies at the Leningrad School of Dance, where she had been in a class taught by M. Romanova. A dancer at the opera and ballet theatres of Erevan, Minsk, and Gorki, among the roles she performed were Giselle, Cinderella, the princess and Maria. From 1969 to 1989, she taught at the Moscow School of Dance. She was invited on several occasions to teach summer courses in Canada and the United States. From 1989 to 1991, she taught at the Tibilisi School of Dance. Among her pupils were L. Ryjova, I.Liepa, N. Ananuchvili, and I. Nioradzé.

TARASSOV, Nikolai Ivanovitch (6 December 1902 – 8 February 1975). Dancer and teacher of repute. Pupil of N. Légat.

After leaving the Moscow School of Dance, he became lead dancer at the Bolshoi. Among the roles he performed were Siegfried *(Swan Lake),* Albert *(Giselle),* Basile *(Don Quixote),* Désiré *(The Sleeping Beauty),* and Jean de Brienne *(Raymonda).*

During his performing career, he taught at the Moscow School of Dance from 1923 to 1960 and directed proficiency classes at the Bolshoi.

A director of the Moscow School of Dance for several years, he was an eminent theorist on the teaching of classical dance, training both dancers and teachers. Between 1962 and 1975, he gave a teaching course for dance teachers at the Institute of Art and Theatre. His most advanced theoretical studies, backed up by extensive teaching experience, were embodied in a series of manuals entitled *The Methodology of Classical Training,* written in collaboration with A. Tchekryguine and V. Lifchuts in 1940, and *Classical Dance (school of male performance),* published in 1975. Among his pupils were famous dancers such as Iou. Jdanov, M. Lavrovski, M. Liepa, Ia. Sekh, A. Lapouri, L. Jdanov, and eminent teachers such as P. Bestov, A. Prokofiev and A. Heroule.

KOJOUKHOVA, Maria Alexéevna (22 February 1897 – 26 November 1959). Ballerina and teacher.

She studied under M. Koulitchevskaia at the Theatre School of St Petersburg before becoming a dancer with the Marie Theatre between 1915 and 1933. She performed the roles of Aurora, the princess *(The Little Hump-backed Horse),* and Svanilda.

Between 1919 and 1933, she taught at the Leningrad School of Dance. From 1933 to 1959, she was one of the principal teachers at the Moscow School of Dance. From 1947, she directed proficiency classes at the Bolshoi, as well as at the Stanislavsky Ballet Music Theatre.

Among her pupils were I. Zoubkovskaia, R. Karelskaia, E. Vlassova, L. Bogomolova, and B. Karieva. She explored in depth and further developed the methodology of the teaching of classical dance.

# List of conventional symbols

1. The positions of the arms are designated by arabic numerals and those of the legs by roman numerals, in accordance with the specialist texts of the day.
2. The poses and positions are indicated by figures (1,2,3...).
3. Attitude settings during transfer from one position to another are designated by letters (A,B,C...).
4. Faults when adopting a position are indicated by a figure and a letter (1A,1B,1C...).
5. Faults in executing a pose are indicated by two figures, one of which is in brackets, for example: 1(1), 1(2), 1(3)...
6. Variations in poses are indicated by a figure and a letter, for example: 1A, 2A...
7. The continuous form of the movement is indicated by a letter, with a figure in brackets, for example: A(1), B(1), C(1)...
8. The techniques used by the teacher to obtain a good arm position are shown, in the first instance by the combination of a letter with a figure "1" (A(1), B(1)...), in the second instance by the combination of a letter with a figure "2" (A(2), B(2)...).
9. The small arrows indicate the direction of movement: A → B, C → D, E → F...
10. Correct: white background • Faults: black background.

2

3

4

1. M. Taglioni
(Flora) in Zéphir
and Flora
by C. Kavos.

2. M. Taglioni.

3. F. Elssler
dancing the
tarantella.
Lithography by
Bouvier.

4. F. Elssler
dancing the
cachucha.
Lithograph
from 1836.

5. C. Grisi
(Giselle).
Drawing by
Brandar.

6. F. Elssler
dancing
cachucha.
Lithograph
by Lakosy.

7. M. Taglioni,
F. Elssler, C. Grisi,
F. Cerrito.

5

6

# Table of Illustrations

**TABLE 1**
*Arrondi* position of the hand – 1, 3.
*Allongée* position of the hand – 2, 4.

**TABLE 2**
The hand in 2nd position.
    correct position – a
    incorrect position – b.

**TABLE 3**
Training the hand at the first stage:
    variations in approach – 1,3; 2,3.

**TABLE 4**
Variations in carriage of the head in classical dance: 1, 2, 3, 4, 5, 6.
    *En face* – 2;
    in profile – 6;
    leaning forward – 5.
Semi-profile:
    leaning slightly forward – 3.
    leaning slightly backward – 4.
    leaning slightly towards the shoulder and looking up – 1.

**TABLE 5**
Movement allowing control of area between the hands in 1st and 3rd positions and to prepare for the imaginary vertical dividing the silhouette in half.
    correct – 1, 2.
    incorrect – 1a, 1b, 2a, 2b.

**TABLE 6**
Arm positions in classical dance:
    *en face* – 1, 2, 3, 4;
    from the back – 1a, 2a, 3a, 4a;
    preparation – 1, 2.
    1st, 2nd position – 3.
    3rd position – 4.

**TABLE 7**
Preparation:
    correct – 1, 2, 3;
    common errors – 1a, 1b, 2a, 2b.

**TABLE 8**
1st position:
    correct – 1, 2.
    common errors – 2a, 2b.

**TABLE 9**
2nd position:
    correct – 1, 2, 3.
    common errors – 2a, 1b, 2b.

**TABLE 10**
3rd position:
    correct – 1, 2, 3;
    common errors – 1a, 1b, 2a, 2b.

**TABLE 11**
Preparatory form of port de bras with elements of raising a → b and lowering c → b → a. Teaching technique allowing pupils to get used to "separating" their arms from their body while they are raising and lowering them – a(1), b(1), c(1).
Teaching technique to instil a feeling for the line during raising and lowering of the arms – a(2), b(2), c(2), d(2), e(2).

**TABLE 12**
Preparatory form of *port de bras* with elements of raising a → b, opening on to b → c and lowering d → e → f.
Teaching technique to work on the exact position of the arms during transfer from one position to another: b(1) → c(1) → d(1) – opening at e(1) → f(1) → g(1) → lowering.

**TABLE 13**
Preparatory form of *port de bras* with elements of raising – a → b → c, d opening → c → d and lowering – e(1) → f(1).
Teaching technique which helps pupils learn to feel the line and position of the arms during the different stages of the movement: a(1), b(1), c(1), d(1), e(1), f(1), g(1).

**TABLE 14**
Preparatory form of *port de bras* with *en dedans* : a, b, c, d, e, f, g.
Teaching technique to develop a sense of the line and exact position of the arms during transfer from one position to another: a → b, c → d, d → e.

**TABLE 15**
Variation of preparatory form of *port de bras* including simultaneous and successive movements: a, b, c, d, e, f, g.

**TABLE 16**
Variation of the preparatory form of *port de bras* using simultaneous and successive movements: a, b, c, d, e, f, g.

**TABLE 17**
Preparatory form of *port de bras* used in class by E.P. Guerdt, with study of poses: a, b, c, d, e, f, g.

**TABLE 18**
Working on elements of the *port de bras,* very important in *adagios, allegros* and turns studied in intermediate and advanced classes: a, b, c, a(1), b(1), c(1).

**TABLE 19**
Positions:
    *en face:* 2;
    *épaulement croisé:* 1;
    *épaulement effacé:* 3;
    preparatory position *à la grande pose croisée:* 1(1);
    preparatory position *à la petite pose croisée:* 1(2);
    preparatory position *à la grande pose effacée* 3(1);
    preparatory position *à la petite pose effacée* 3(2);

**TABLE 20**
The *croisé avant* pose:
    toe pointed on the floor: 1, raised to 90 degrees: 2
Variation of the *croisé avant* pose: 2a, 2b, 2c, 2d.
    common faults: 1(1), 1(2), 1(3).

**TABLE 21**
The *croisé arrière* pose:
    toe pointed on the floor: 1, raised to 90 degrees: 2.
Variations of the *croisé arrière* pose: 2a, 2b, 2c, 2d.
    common faults: 1(1), 1(2), 1(3).

**TABLE 22**
The *croisé avant* pose:
    toe pointed on the floor: 1, raised to 90 degrees: 2.
Variations of the *croisé avant* pose: 2a, 2b, 2c, 2d.
    common faults: 1(1), 1(2), 1(3).

**TABLE 23**
The *effacé arrière* pose:
    toe pointed on the floor: 1, raised to 90 degrees: 2.
Variations of the *effacé arrière* pose: 2a, 2b, 2c, 2d.
    common faults: 1(1), 1(2), 1(3).

*V. Vassilyev and
Y. Maximova
in the ballet
"Spartacus".*

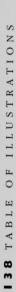